# HELPING PARENTS IN DISPUTE

*To Bill and Kath*

# Helping Parents in Dispute

Child-centred mediation at county court

GREG MANTLE
*Anglia Polytechnic University*

Routledge
Taylor & Francis Group

LONDON AND NEW YORK

First published 2001 by Ashgate Publishing

Reissued 2018 by Routledge
2 Park Square, Milton Park, Abingdon, Oxon OX14 4RN
711 Third Avenue, New York, NY 10017, USA

*Routledge is an imprint of the Taylor & Francis Group, an informa business*

Notice:
Product or corporate names may be trademarks or registered trademarks, and are used only for identification and explanation without intent to infringe.

Publisher's Note
The publisher has gone to great lengths to ensure the quality of this reprint but points out that some imperfections in the original copies may be apparent.

Disclaimer
The publisher has made every effort to trace copyright holders and welcomes correspondence from those they have been unable to contact.

A Library of Congress record exists under LC control number: 2001091616


ISBN 13: 978-1-138-73480-7 (hbk)
ISBN 13: 978-1-138-73477-7 (pbk)
ISBN 13: 978-1-315-18698-6 (ebk)

# Contents

# Foreword

Mediation and conciliation in various guises have been an accepted and welcome step in private law family proceedings for about 15 years in the Essex County Courts. In my judicial role I have, of course, taken a keen interest in the development of 'alternative dispute resolution' over this period and am very pleased to be able to preface this important new work on the subject.

The research study on which this book is partly based progressed under the watchful and intrigued eye of a working party of family court welfare officers experienced in family mediation, a solicitor, judge and assistant chief probation officer. The research had been commissioned by Essex Probation Service who asked two very straightforward questions: how long do the agreements we broker last and how do the parents rate us?

The responding parents gave thoughtful and revealing answers. These have been analysed and categorised by Greg Mantle and themselves provoke further questions to those responsible for the mediation services offered. This comes at an important stage within family law proceedings as publicly funded litigation diminishes and the Family Court Welfare Service is re-aligned to CAFCASS. Being able to deliver a 'product' that will be both attractive to users and cost effective will be a priority for the new service. As a result, this book offers an important and timely appraisal of current mediation practice, as experienced by parents who have been in dispute over contact or residence arrangements for their children.

Many of the study findings will be of interest to the architects and deliverers of the new service. For instance, there appears to be an overwhelming desire for an agreement which is 'enforceable'; parents rarely seem to trust each other in these situations and it might be that the long held notion that agreement should mean 'no order' may have to be statutorily re-visited. However, the overall value of the philosophy of mediation is reinforced and as one mother said:

If it can keep people out of court which is most anxiety provoking then it must be a good thing to try to do. I was terrified at thinking about going to court which I have never done in my life before.

Although the research is local to a relatively small court catchment area the lessons and questions raised will have a larger impact for all such services, whether in the private or public arena. The providers need to know what happens to settlements in the short and medium term, and the experiences of parents as they struggle to put agreements into practice.

Elizabeth Silverwood-Cope
District Court Judge
Spring 2001

# Acknowledgements

Many people have helped in the writing of this book. In particular, I want to record my appreciation for the assistance and stewardship of Liz Cope, Sue Lowden, Silvia Ould, Jose Rowe, Alan Critchley, Phil Gould and Ray Shaffer. Lesley Dobreé and Kate Atherton ensured that time was made available, and Gwynn Davis provided encouragement and generous welcome.

Many thanks are due to Jill, Erica, Isaac and Robbie, for their enduring support and patience, and to Avalon Associates of Chelmsford for final checking, formatting and preparation of camera-ready copy.

A very special debt is owed to the parents and carers who took part in the Essex study.

# List of Abbreviations

| | |
|---|---|
| ACOP | Association of Chief Officers of Probation |
| ADR | Alternative Dispute Resolution |
| BCS | British Crime Survey |
| CAFCASS | Children and Family Court Advisory Support Service |
| CSA | Child Support Agency |
| CPU | Conciliation Project Unit |
| EPS | Essex Probation Service |
| EFCS | Essex Family Court Service |
| FCDRC | Family and Community Dispute Research Centre |
| FCS | Family Court Service |
| FCWS | Family Court Welfare Service |
| FMA | Family Mediators Association |
| FPSC | Family Policy Studies Centre |
| GALRO | Guardian *ad Litem* and Reporting Officer |
| HMSO | Her Majesty's Stationery Office |
| NFM | National Family Mediation |
| ONS | Office for National Statistics |

# 1 Introduction

Family mediation is a relatively new development, even when its immediate predecessor, 'family conciliation', is taken into account. Nevertheless, over the past three decades, the settling of disputes between parents by 'informal' methods, rather than via more traditional, legalistic routes, has rapidly come to prominence. There are at least two crucial caveats to such statements: first, the emergence of family mediation in the West may, in fact, be traced back to much earlier times; and, second, mediation has been practised in other parts of the world as far back as the fifth century BC (Parkinson, 1997, pp.2–3).

Family dissolution is frequently associated with high levels of antagonism and conflict between parents, and the space to find mutually-acceptable arrangements, as to where children will live and when they will be able to spend time with their non-resident parent, may become considerably reduced. The importance of being able to reach a settlement on such matters is widely recognised, as are the consequences for children being exposed to parental conflict pre- and post-separation (Rodgers and Pryor, 1998, pp.41–42). The need for some form of external intervention – the provision of information, support services, counselling or dispute resolution via the courts, therapy or mediation – is therefore readily apparent, although the focus in the UK has to date been mainly on providing specialist services to parents rather than to children. The direct involvement of children, affected by the separation of their parents, in the processes aimed at achieving agreement on residence and contact arrangements remains largely undeveloped, although there are indications that this state of affairs may be changing (Robinson, 1999).

Mediation has become an attractive option to more formal methods of dispute resolution in a wide range of fields, including: criminal justice, bringing victims and offenders together (Marshall and Merry, 1990; Wright 1996; Strang and Braithwaite, 2000; Wynne, 2000); peer mediation in schools (Hartop, 1996; Bitel and Rolls, 2000; Lawrence, 2000); and industrial and commercial sectors (Donahey, 1995; Newman, 2000; Reynolds, 2000). There is evidently considerable value in being able to set family mediation within this wider frame of reference but there is also a need to differentiate it from related, informal procedures that may be employed. 'Negotiation' is usually understood as a way of solving conflicts by the disputants themselves – parents often reach an agreement without involving solicitors or mediators. 'Arbitration' may be defined as involving a neutral third party who, having heard all sides to the dispute, provides a final decision. This is similar to the process of legalistic 'adjudication' – sometimes referred to as 'litigation', although this latter term may perhaps be more helpfully defined as the act of bringing or contesting a lawsuit. The difference between arbitration and legalistic adjudication is that the former, although structured, may be much less regulated than the courtroom, with its set procedures and exacting rules of evidence. 'Mediation' may thus be conceptualised as a means of helping parties in dispute reach a settlement, the terms of which are decided by the disputants rather than by the mediator(s). Mediators do not expect to adjudicate, rather she or he manages negotiations between, usually, two parties who are in dispute. However, disputants, especially those who are unfamiliar with the role of mediation, frequently do expect mediators to 'judge' and this proclivity is recognised within the professional literature as a potential obstacle to proceedings (Haynes, 1993, p.6).

Mediation may also be distanced conceptually from 'therapy' and, in the context of family court dispute resolution, this produces a helpful triadic frame of mediation, judicial intervention and therapeutic approaches. Mediation may thus be regarded as an alternative to therapy as well as an alternative to legalistic adjudication. It is important to acknowledge that family court practitioners have a long-standing tradition of employing methods rooted in social work and psychodynamics in their work with families: their understanding of, and opinions about, mediation will therefore be set within this practice heritage and broader assumptive world. Some practitioners have argued for the greater use of therapeutic approaches in cases where mediation appears inappropriate because of the level of antagonism between parents (Waite, 2000). In such situations, judicial intervention is the norm, involving calls to the disputants to 'put the child's needs first' and, possibly, the imposition of various discomforts and sanctions. Protagonists of therapy take the view that such a legalistic approach is doomed to failure because it addresses only the symptoms of the conflict, rather than the underlying causes: mediation, even if possible, would likewise be deemed too superficial.

Positioning mediation within this analytical framework, as an alternative to both judicial and therapeutic responses, readily brings to mind the potential utility of a political metaphor for understanding organisational behaviour within the family court environment (Morgan, 1986, pp.141–198). Decisions about which of the three available options for dispute resolution to employ for a particular case would thence be perceived as having political, as well as 'professional', dimensions. The query 'Who is mediation for?' thus begs a number of key questions about the relative powers and accountabilities of the various stakeholder groups concerned: for example, practitioners might be tempted to categorise a couple as unsuitable for mediation, perhaps with an accompanying rationale emphasising the level of antagonism between the two parties, in order to enhance their 'success rate' within an organisational context that stipulates targets and standards for performance. The organisational politics of family dispute resolution and, relatedly, of family mediation has, to date, been afforded little attention in the literature.

Of course, even within the context of family disputes, the term 'mediation' has been applied to a wide range of different practices. There are many types of mediation. There is also disagreement about whether or not particular practices of dispute resolution should actually be classified as 'mediation'. Writing about mediation thus runs the risk of over-generalisation and it is therefore important to define as clearly and as early as possible the parameters of the work. This is a book about one specific type of family mediation, namely 'county court dispute resolution', that is carried out on court premises by family court service officers and, although some wider relevance seems inevitable, no general application nor pertinence is uncritically proffered.

## Characteristics of County Court Mediation

Mediation has two main forms: 'child-centred', which is concerned solely with assisting parents to make arrangements about, mainly, residence and contact for their children – and 'all issues' or comprehensive mediation, which also includes financial and property matters. This essay is concerned solely with child-centred mediation that ensues on county court premises and follows receipt of an application for an order under section 8 of the *Children Act 1989*. Most of the applications included in the Essex study (see below) had been made by a natural parent of the child/children concerned: about two thirds of 'couples' had been married, while about one third had not been married, but had cohabited. While the focus of the work is on 'county courts', it is acknowledged that mediation also takes place under the auspices of family proceedings courts. Similarly, the specification of location – 'county court premises' – is made within a recognisance that mediation may also take place elsewhere.

Mediation may also be classified by the number of sessions or meetings that are offered in order to reach a settlement. Lindstein and Meteyard (1996) distinguish four such types: single consultation, short-term, medium-term and long-term. The definitions offered by the authors for these categories are difficult to decipher from the text but it is possible to say that by 'short-term' they mean two sessions. Lindstein and Meteyard respond to the apparent conceptual proximity of single consultation and short-term as follows:

> Two sessions may seem like a very short series and hardly much different from a single consultative session. But in fact, agreeing to meet a second time can make a decisive difference and may signify the start of a constructive process (p.39).

This book addresses the practice of employing a single consultation in order to resolve a dispute between parents. Although a number of cases in the Essex study did involve further mediation meetings, the research focus is on the initial session, because that is where an agreement had been reached. Subsequent settlements reached by the couple, during the study time period, were not treated as constituting a survey 'case' within the research frame.

Mediation has been and is provided by a range of different agencies and traverses a number of different professional disciplines. Some mediation services operate independently, others are provided by charitable bodies, and some are statutory. Some mediators are counsellors, others are lawyers, perhaps with a particular interest in the resolution of financial disputes. Many are family court service officers employed by area probation services, at the time of writing, although soon to become members of the Children and Family Court Advisory Support Service (CAFCASS). This book is concerned with the mediation services provided at county courts by family court officers.

The number of mediators involved in any one session offers a further way of categorising practice: co-mediation, the employment of two practitioners, may usefully be distinguished from sole reliance on one mediator. Having two mediators present, one female and one male, may be understood as a way of avoiding a 'gender-imbalance'. Furthermore, in cases of co-mediation, both mediators may have similar roles or they may have different roles – co-mediation may embrace mediators from different disciplines, say counselling and the law, or both mediators may come from the same profession. This essay examines the use of sole and co-mediation by family court service officers.

Finally, it is important to acknowledge the widespread acceptance that mediation is, and that it should be, entirely voluntary. In other words, parents should not be obliged to undertake mediation: put sharply, mediation and coercion may be regarded as incompatible. However, in reality, 'mediation' can be formally required: Robinson (1999, p.133) refers to services in California, for example, that operate on such a non-voluntary basis and she usefully points out that much of the extant research in this field has been conducted in the United States. It is important therefore, given the international audience of this book, to state that the work is concerned solely with voluntary mediation, in the sense that parents are not formally required to submit to it. However, the issue of participation is much broader. There is a need to go beyond the limits of 'formal requirement' because parents may well feel that they 'ought' to take their respective disputes to mediation, even though no such stipulation exists. Some may even fear the predicted reaction of officialdom should they not do so. These are key sensitivities, bringing user/consumer constructions of the basis of mediation to the foreground of consideration and prompting a set of searching questions. Who, for example, do mediators represent? What powers are they perceived to command? Does their heralded association with 'court' announce special privilege? How might refusal be met and what consequences could ensue? The pertinence of such questions has been sharpened by recent developments such as the provision of compulsory 'information meetings' under section 13 of the *Family Law Act 1996* (Cretney, 2000, p.70; McCarthy, 2000). At time of writing, this section of the Act has yet to be implemented, although pilot schemes have been instigated in order to establish how best to deliver the meetings. Piloting is also underway in relation to section 29 of the 1996 Act, amending section 15 of the *Legal Aid Act 1988*, so as to make eligibility for legal aid conditional on the applicant having attended a meeting with a mediator, in order to assess the suitability of mediation. Mediators have argued strongly that this requirement does not mean that mediation will no longer be voluntary in such cases (Stevenson, 2000, p.40) and, in a formal sense, this is probably accurate. However, Section 29 includes the following precept:

> ...if mediation does appear suitable, to help the person applying for representation to decide whether instead to apply for mediation...

and much would appear to hang on the interpretation of the verb '*help*' therein. Clearly, the emphasis for the mediator undertaking the assessment has been placed on encouraging a decision for, rather than against, mediation. Disputants may therefore feel under no little pressure to opt in favour of mediation. As yet, the available empirical evidence from the pilots suggests that this is unlikely to be happening: the vast majority of people attending an information meeting do not proceed to mediation (80 per cent – Davis, 1999, p.631; 93 per cent – McCarthy, 2000, p.553). Nevertheless, the issue of voluntariness will no doubt continue to feature prominently in mediation discourse. Similarly, the relationship between mode of funding and 'choice' must remain a matter of public concern. As Liebmann (2000, p.13) points out, wealthier people may retain the options of mediation or employing a lawyer, while poorer individuals may be 'encouraged' to go to mediation. Men, who are more likely than their ex-partners to be able to afford both legal representation and mediation fees, are also (further) advantaged.

In regard to the Essex study population, it is not possible to provide figures pertaining to the proportions of mediation disputants respectively state- and self-funded. However, it is possible to say that, on the basis of the interview and postal survey data collected, some parents had been financed via legal aid while others had been self-funded. In a formal sense, all disputants attended mediation on a voluntary basis, although the research data suggests that some may have felt obliged to participate for one reason or another.

**Introducing the Chapters**

Chapter 1 defines the focus of the book and considers how the need for mediation might be gauged. Chapter 2 reviews traditional wisdom about the significance and effectiveness of mediation, and argues the case for an expansion of the current measures of efficacy to include the duration of mediation settlements. The question of whether or not agreements stand the test of time has, to date, received little attention in professional and academic literatures: chapter 2 not only sheds some light on why this omission may have occurred but also begins to pave the way for widespread recognition of the 'persistence of settlement' as a valid criterion of success in mediation practice. The assumption made by central government, that court-based mediation is less likely to be effective than services otherwise delivered, is also shown to be worthy of considerable circumspection.

Chapter 3 takes a look at mediation from the father's perspective. The issue of contact between children and their fathers is presently of enormous interest and debate, and this chapter makes a substantial contribution through an exploration of the views and preoccupying concerns of male service users in regard to mediation outcomes and processes. The presumption that contact must be beneficial is critically examined and the chapter concludes that the lack of a clear picture of what productive, post-divorce fatherhood might look like is unhelpful to parents and to mediators. Chapter 3 also addresses the case of resident fathers and points to the need for further study of the utility of traditional concepts of 'mothering' in the area of sole male parenting. Relatedly, a search for the rationale of the non-resident mother's right to contact is commended.

Chapter 4 considers the safety and utility of mediation in cases involving intimate partner violence, drawing upon the views of women service users in the contexts of shared waiting areas and seating arrangements during mediation. Women who have suffered violence are likely to feel very anxious about meeting their ex-partner and this chapter relates a series of harrowing experiences that serve to pose sharp questions for current mediation practice, especially the use of confrontational, 'face-to-face' seating formats during sessions. The acceptability of the notion of 'domestic violence', commonplace in professional and academic discourse, is also revisited.

Chapter 5 takes a look at the parts played by lawyers and judges in mediation, through the eyes of the parents who are seeking solutions to their contact and residence disputes. The consequences for mediators of only one of the two parents being legally represented are addressed. Many lawyers continue to be ambivalent about the position of mediation in divorce proceedings and chapter 5 considers why this should be so. The ramifications of mediating within a court ambience are also considered: notions and effects of formality and gravity are reviewed.

Chapter 6 examines key contemporary assumptions concerning 'best practice' in mediation. The phenomenon of co-mediation is scrutinised. Attention is paid to the preparation of parents for their mediation meeting and to the expectations that they bring. The setting and policing of 'rules of engagement' are reviewed in the light of user testimony. Chapter 6 also addresses the professionalisation of mediation work, its pursuit of 'neutrality' and detachment, and how such developments may be perceived by those on the receiving end of practice. Important questions are raised about the delivery of service to minority sections of the community. Finally, the involvement of the child in mediation is examined and doubts are raised about the prospect of hearing the voice of the child in present county court practice.

In conclusion, chapter 7 offers an evaluation of current county court mediation policy and practice, with an eye to the early years of the new unified agency, CAFCASS, launched in April 2001. The efficacy of child-centred mediation in this setting is reconsidered and assumptions made by government are critically revisited. Finally, county court practice is reviewed within the conceptual context of informalism.

## The Essex Study

Although a comprehensive account of the Essex study research is provided in Appendix 1, it may be helpful to give a brief outline of the study at this introductory point in the writing. A large-scale postal survey of parents who had reached full agreement at county court mediation was undertaken during the period from 1 October 1999 to 30 September 2000, the primary ambitions of the work being to evaluate user/consumer perspectives on the significance, duration, outcomes and effects of those agreements, and to consider potential implications for policy and practice. The research approach was to attempt 'complete coverage', rather than to sample: all parents and carers reaching full agreement at mediation sessions, conducted at the four county courts in Essex, over a period of 12 months, were initially included. A number of potential participants in the study were not contactable but a total of 722 was eventually realised. A respectable response rate of 48 per cent was achieved, producing 65 paired replies – that is, responses from both parents – from a total of 345 completed questionnaires. Statistical analyses were undertaken using the SPSS programme and the findings published in Mantle (2000, 2001a and 2001b).

In Appendix 2, a series of case studies is presented, based on accounts of both parents for each case, set against background information taken from available documentation. Although the studies will be of general interest, they may be particularly apposite for mediator training purposes. The data have a special significance given the dearth of comparable material previously to hand. Because of low return rates, earlier surveys have generated only small absolute numbers and proportions of 'paired replies'.

In order to avoid any possible confusion, it is necessary to announce that the descriptor 'Essex' is used in the text to define a geographical area, the county of Essex. The study was undertaken under the auspices of Anglia Polytechnic University and has no connection whatsoever with the University of Essex.

## Mediation, Family Law and Informalism

> Mediation, or conciliation, as it was more commonly known, was often discussed as an alternative dispute resolution, but within the shadow of the law (Walker *et al.*, 1994, p.3).

Robinson (1999) provides a succinct history of family mediation, from its early foundations in the Finer Committee Report (1974) through to the (continuing) implementation of the *Family Law Act 1996*. She suggests that mediation, formerly known as conciliation, can usefully be regarded as lying on the boundary of law and counselling/psychotherapy (p.128). The overall aim of mediation is to help parents to manage the consequences of their divorce or separation, by reaching agreements on, or reducing conflict over, key issues connected with finances, property and/or the child or children concerned. Mediation needs to be distinguished from reconciliation, the search for a way to maintain the marriage or partnership.

On a broader canvas, mediation can be understood as one expression of 'informalism' – the move away from litigation and adjudication as a way of resolving disputes – so it is possible to place it alongside other projects such as 'arbitration' and 'negotiation' in industrial and commercial contexts, and public provisions for hearing complaints, grievances and claims of discrimination. The 'move away' from having recourse to the law leads to the notion of 'alternative dispute resolution': mediation can thus be made sense of as one form of 'ADR'. However, this conceptualisation has received considerable criticism on the grounds that it: (1) may foster an assumption that informality is always 'better' than more traditional methods; (2) suggests that all mediation is uniformly 'informal'; and (3) that it erroneously implies a complete separation from the law.

On the first of these three points, there is a need to be clear on the precise criteria by which mediation is deemed to be superior and to consider carefully evidence for and against the assertion of ascendancy on each specific count. The arrival of family mediation may be seen as a reaction against the 'adversarial' nature of traditional court-based approaches to the resolution of disputes: the key assumption being that such modes actually increase antagonism between parents. Thus, it is necessary to both review evidence for and against the claim that litigation 'makes matters worse', in this regard, and to test the assertion that mediation offers a better option. Chapter 2 provides a detailed discussion of the search for measures of effectiveness, while chapter 5 revisits the question of how legalistic routes may affect disputant relationships.

The second ground for criticism acts as a reminder both that mediation may be experienced differently by the various actors within it, and that the different forms of mediation may vary in their relative 'informality' – county court mediation, provided by family court officers on court premises, for example, might be experienced by parents as a formal, even legalistic process. Similarly, mediation delivered by lawyers, family court officers and counsellors, respectively, may be received very differently.

On the final point raised, it is important to recognise that, although it may, indeed, be useful to contrast mediation with legalistic approaches to dispute resolution, to suggest an impermeable distinction between the two would be misleading. After all, mediation ensues within proceedings under the *Children Act 1989* – applications made for contact, residence, specific issue and prohibited steps orders – and adjudication frequently follows unsuccessful mediation sessions. However, the relationship is not always so straightforward, as exemplified by the following discussion of confidentiality and legal privilege. Mediation meetings may be described as 'privileged', as distinct from other meetings involving family court officers such as 'directions appointments' (Home Office, 1994, pp.7–9) that are not privileged. In broad terms, a privileged meeting is confidential, meaning that what is said during mediation may only be reported to the court if both parents, or parties, agree. However, there is, in fact, no statutory privilege in England and Wales ensuring confidentiality (Parkinson, 1997, p.16), so that 'case law' from Court of Appeal rulings has to suffice, while, in Scotland, section 1(1) of the *Civil Evidence (Family Mediation) Act 1995* provides the statutory underpinning for confidentiality in mediation.

The aims, benefits, limitations and processes of family mediation have been widely discussed (Irving and Benjamin, 1995; Parkinson, 1997; Roberts, 1997; Stevenson, 2000) and the intention is not to repeat the detail of such discussions here. Chapter 2 provides an account of 'what works' in mediation, relating effectiveness to its various, declared ambitions, while chapter 6 examines a number of specific mediation practices and their supporting rationales.

## The Need for Mediation: Divorce, Separation and Cohabitation

> Over the past twenty years the number of divorces greatly increased, drastically changing divorce law. Most states now have a form of no-fault divorce allowing the parties, and not the courts, to decide to end a marriage (Loeb, 1999, p.581).

Loeb makes a link between the increased likelihood of divorce, its acceptance as a common experience in the lives of many members of society and the shift away from courts and the law. The idea that couples should be able to conclude their partnership, without judicial intervention, has achieved widespread support and the popularity of mediation – as a way of resolving disputes without recourse to the law – may justifiably be associated with this belief. Other changes in family demography may also have had some impact: the deferral of timing in family formation over recent decades (Irwin, 1999, p.31) means that parents may be expected to be more mature and able to make responsible decisions. Later marriage, increased female participation in the employment and higher education sectors, and the greater efficacy of contraception have all played a part in delaying family commencement. In England and Wales, because of later marriage, parents who divorce now tend to be older: the average age rose from 40.2 years for men and 37.7 years for women, in 1997, to 40.9 and 38.4 years, respectively, in 1999. However, a more exacting examination produces a picture that is far more complicated: Kline Pruett and Jackson (1999, p.284), for example, state that, in the United States and Canada, parents with young children constitute the fastest growing part of the divorcing population, with perhaps 20 per cent of all ten to eleven year olds having experienced parental separation before their fifth birthday. In other words, family commencement may have been deferred, while family dissolution now tends to occur earlier. Kline Pruett and Jackson also state that families with younger children constitute the largest group using court-related services, citing findings from research in California that children aged between one and nine, with a median age of seven years, are more highly represented among court mediation families than in the general population (Depner *et al.*, 1995).

In England and Wales there were 145,200 divorces in 1998, more than 13 divorces per thousand married couples, figures comparable with those of Denmark and Sweden, although much lower than those in the United States (Rodgers and Pryor, 1998, p.4). Although the figures are high, their interpretation deserves some considerable caution, especially given the politicised nature of public discourse on the question of divorce. So, it is true that the number of divorces has effectively doubled since 1971, but the total has, in fact, fallen from 158,700 in 1991 to its current level. The most recent figures show that the decline in divorce has continued, with a total of 144,600 divorces in 1999: this means that less than 1.3 per cent of the married population underwent divorce, the lowest proportion since 1990. Nevertheless, it is estimated that, should present rates persist, more than one third of all new marriages will end within 20 years and four out of every ten will eventually terminate in divorce.

Of course, not all divorces or marital separations involve dependent children and, for the purposes of predicting the need for mediation – especially child-centred services – it is important to know how many do include such children. The number of divorces in England and Wales involving couples with children under 16 years of age peaked in 1993, at 95,000. In 1998, about 151,000 children experienced divorce between their parents, compared with 176,000 in 1993 and 82,000 in 1971 (Office for National Statistics [ONS], 2000a, table 2.22, p.46). However, the proportion of divorcing couples who have children under 16 has remained relatively constant since the mid-1980s, at approximately 55 per cent.

There is also a need in this context to be able to predict the ages of children most frequently affected by divorce and separation. Older children, for example, are more likely to have their own views on contact and residence arrangements: many teenagers simply 'vote with their feet'. In 1998, about one in four children affected by divorce were under five years old and about seven in ten were aged less than ten years. Almost one in four children born in 1979 were likely to have been affected by divorce before they had reached 16 years of age. If current trends continue, 19 per cent of children born to married couples will experience divorce by the age of ten and 28 per cent by the age of 16 (Rodgers and Pryor, 1998, p.4, who acknowledge that theses figures are based on an underestimate of the real rate of family breakdown because they exclude the separation of cohabiting couples).

Despite the decline in marriage over the past four decades, the institution continues to retain an attraction: although the total number of marriages in Great Britain has decreased over the period 1971–1997, from

447,000 to 302,000, the number of remarriages has increased from 67,000 to 128,000 over the same period of time. Of course, part of this increase can be accounted for by the higher divorce rate – in other words, there are more dissolved first marriages and, consequently, more divorced people who may remarry. Nevertheless, the maxim 'once bitten, twice shy' appears to have limited application in view of the rate of remarriage. More generally, support for the institution of marriage may be drawn from the fact that four-fifths of dependent children still live in a family with two parents, and nine out of ten of those parents are married (Family Policy Studies Centre, 2000, p.4).

Much of the mediation literature appears to focus exclusively on cases arising from divorce and marital separation: cohabitation is frequently left unmentioned or quietly subsumed within cases of 'separation' – see, for example, Robinson (1999). Parkinson (1997) alerts us to the priority given to counselling and mediation services for 'married' couples whose relationship has broken down and reminds us that:

> Unmarried couples also need help when they separate and separation is deeply distressing for children, irrespective of whether their parents are married. Publicly funded mediation services need to be widely and readily available to unmarried as well as married couples – as they are in New Zealand (p.392).

This apparent lack of attention can be placed within a much wider and long-standing context of neglect. Family law has, for many years, been concerned solely with marriage, its breakdown (separation) and dissolution (divorce). Cohabitation has been regarded as decidedly second-best as a foundation for family formation. As Cretney (2000) points out, there is no automatic entitlement to the legal rights of marriage for partners who live as 'common law spouses' (p.10). Also, the mother and father of a child born outside wedlock do not share the same entitlements: only the mother has parental responsibility for the child (section 2(2) of the *Children Act 1989*), although the father may subsequently acquire it by making an agreement with the mother or by making application to court under section 8 of the *Children Act 1989* for either a residence or parental responsibility order. Even the most cursory inspection of the *Family Law Act 1996* indicates that the exclusive concern with marriage continues, arguably that the preoccupation has strengthened. The general principles underlying Parts II and III of the Act focus entirely on marriage, marital breakdown and to violence within the context of marriage: principle 1(a) states that the institution of marriage is to be supported, which, as Freeman

(1996, p.9) says, inevitably prioritises marriage over its alternatives. The text reads as if cohabitation had not even featured in the deliberations leading to the Act's construction. Similarly, heterosexual relationships are also elevated over lesbian and gay partnerships.

Of the relevant cases in the Essex study, 68 per cent involved parents who were still married, or who had been married, to each other, and 32 per cent involved parents who had not been married to each other. In other words, about two thirds of mediation cases were between parents who had been married and one third were between parents who had cohabited. These are important findings, given the absence of similar data from previous research in this field. It is now possible to state, for example, that family court services do provide mediation to both status groupings in society. Furthermore, the proportions appear to be within the expected range: official statistics show that the proportion of all non-married women aged 18 to 49 who were cohabiting in Great Britain was 29 per cent in 1998–1999 (ONS, 2000a, p.40). On the issue of mediation for homosexual partnerships, there were no such cases within the total of 448 notified to the research team during the one year study period.

Gauging the future need for mediation services must involve an awareness of key social trends and, certainly, the shift away from marriage, towards cohabitation, has been pronounced over the past two decades or so. The proportion of women cohabiting has increased nearly threefold, from 11 per cent in 1979 to 29 per cent in 1998–1999 and it is estimated that there were about 1.6 million couples cohabiting in England and Wales in 1996. The peak age group for cohabitation among unmarried women in Great Britain during 1998–1999 was 25–29 years, with 39 per cent of women cohabiting, while for men it was 30–34 years, with 44 per cent of men cohabiting. The peak age group for women cohabiting is also the group most likely to give birth, with 102 live births per thousand, compared with 74 and 90 live births per thousand for, respectively, the immediately proximate age groups 20–24 and 30–34 years. Almost four in ten live births in Great Britain during 1998 occurred outside marriage, more than four times the proportion in 1974, and most of the increase since the late 1980s has been to cohabiting couples. In 1998, about four fifths of births outside marriage were jointly registered by both parents, three quarters of these births were to parents living at the same address (ONS, 2000a, pp.40–43).

A different development, worthy of note in predicting the need for mediation, is the increase in lone parenting over the past three decades. Before the mid-1980s, much of the rise in lone parenthood was due to divorce, while, more recently, single lone motherhood – defined as never married, not cohabiting and with children – has grown at a faster rate. In 1972, 6 per cent of dependent children in Great Britain lived in lone mother families (1 per cent in lone father units) while, by 1998–1999, this figure had increased almost fourfold to 23 per cent (only 2 per cent in lone father families) (ONS, 2000a, p.46). In 1971, there were just over half a million lone parents, with around one million dependent children: by the mid-1990s, there were 1.6 million lone parents, raising 2.8 million dependent children (Family Policy Studies Centre, 2000, pp.3–4). The proportions for 'separated or divorced' – that is, still married or previously married to the other natural parent – lone parents show a similar rate of increase, from 4.4 per cent at the beginning of the 1970s to just under 13 per cent in 1994. Those living with a separated or divorced lone father rose from about 0.5 per cent to one per cent over the same period (Rodgers and Pryor, 1998, p.4).

The growth in single lone motherhood presents something of a conundrum in this predictive context. Superficially, it might be interpreted as a sign that mediation services could be scaled downwards in the future, because there will be fewer applications from fathers for contact, parental responsibility and other section 8 orders. However, the definition of single lone motherhood offered above leaves out a significant category of women, those who had cohabited in the past but never married the natural father of their child or children. Furthermore, the proportion of women in this category is likely to be increasing, given the more general shift away from marriage. From this vantage point, the demand for mediation may be much steadier or even increase over the coming decades. Recent research shows a sharp division between marriage and cohabitation in terms of the persistence of a relationship: 36 per cent of children born to cohabiting parents are still looked after by both parents by the time they reach the age of 16 years, compared to 70 per cent of children born to married parents. The study also states that children whose parents do not marry are much more likely to reach adulthood with emotional and psychological problems (Ermisch, 2000).

However, such findings need to be set within wider discussions around the repercussions of poverty: after all, marriage is an expensive sojourn and, therefore, the antecedents of both cohabitation and relationship breakdown may be relative impoverishment. It is also known that divorce rates are higher among lower socio-economic groups (Kuh and Maclean, 1990; Elliot *et al.*, 1993). There are firm indications that poverty has increased sharply over the past two decades: research by

Bradshaw *et al.* (2000) suggests that, between 1983 and 1999, the proportion of households in poverty rose from 14 to 24 per cent, nearly one quarter of all those in Britain, and the authors point out the damaging effects of 'being poor' on family relationships, health, education and employment. Furthermore, the relationship between parental separation and children's adjustment is far from simple (see Rodgers and Pryor, 1998, pp.18–32, for a comparison of separated and intact families) and there is no evidence to suggest that all children are disadvantaged by the parting of their parents.

Finally, in this section, it is important to acknowledge that any appraisal worth its salt of the likely demand for mediation must embrace the issue of complexity, as well as the number, of cases. In order to illustrate this point, it may be helpful to compare and contrast the mediation of two cases, the first involving one child aged, shall we say, one year, and the second involving three children, aged two, ten and fourteen years. Evidently, the scope for dispute between the parents is much greater in the second scenario and, as a consequence, the 'demand' on the mediator is likely to be increased. 'Complexity', then, needs to be taken into consideration and there are a number of aspects of family mediation cases that may be associated with this broad variable. The number of children in the family is certainly one important concern. So too is the age-range of sibling groups: consider, for example, the above situation comprising three children of very different ages – contact arrangements for the two year old may be radically different from those necessary for the fourteen year old child, who will have a view on what she or he wants to transpire. The relative complexity of a case may also involve the relationships between the children concerned – natural, half- or step-siblings – and the presence of 'other children' in the reordered family network whose needs and wishes may have to be recognised.

Official statistics on children in families of divorced couples provide pointers for predicting the possible complexity of caseloads, although the absence of similar figures for children in families of (dissolved) cohabitation urges caution. Within the 80,476 families of divorce in 1998 involving at least one child under 16, there were 50,129 children, an average of 1.866, or about 2 children per divorce (ONS, 2000b, table 4.10). On the basis of such calculation, mediators might therefore expect to work primarily with cases including more than one child. Of course, the average figure tells us little about the real distribution but it does suggest that cases involving one child are less likely. However, an analysis of data from the Essex study initially produces a different picture. Data from 448 families, concerning a total of 754 children, were available from family court service records and of these families 50 per cent had one (study) child only, while 36 per cent had two and 15 per cent had three or more children (see chapter six for further discussion of the resourcing issues linked to the direct and indirect involvement of children in mediation). The average number of children per case, at 1.68, is significantly lower than might be expected from the national figure. The difference could be a reflection of local variations concealed within the average figure for England and Wales, although the size of the gap, at almost 0.2, suggests that fewer dependent children are brought up within disordered families of cohabitation than those of marriage, given that the Essex sample includes both types of unit. And, indeed, this appears to be the case: the average number of children per divorced or divorcing couple coming to mediation in Essex is 1.853, satisfyingly similar to the national figure, while the average for ex-cohabitants is much lower, at 1.325. So, for this group of couples, 76 per cent had one child, 17 per cent had two and 7 per cent had three or more children concerned with the mediation. The corresponding figures for divorced or divorcing couples going to mediation are, respectively, 38 per cent, 44 per cent and 18 per cent. Needless to say, the differences between the two groupings are substantial, with the cohabitation families being much more likely to have one dependent child. However, there are dangers in dealing exclusively in such aggregated data: it is also vitally important that key differences subsumed within the average figures are properly recognised. For example, the overall proportions given above for families of cohabitation might be taken to mean that all such units were short-term liaisons that each produced one child. In reality, there are many individual cases of long-term partnerships involving three, four or five dependent children. The relative complexity of such cases may be high and as a corollary the demand on mediation services may also be increased.

Finally, although average family size has shown a significant reduction since the 1960s, the figure has, in fact, been increasing over the past decade, from 1.78 in 1988 to 1.87 in 1998. However, the rate of increase has been much slower of late with a slight fall from 1996–1997. In 1998, 30,967 divorcing couples had only one dependent child out of a total of 80,476 couples, a proportion of just over 38 per cent, much lower than the aggregate figure from the Essex study of 50 per cent but identical to the proportion for families of divorce. In the same year, 34,207 couples had two dependent children, giving a percentage of 42.5, proximate to the Essex figure of 44 per cent: 15,302 couples had three dependent children, or 19 per cent of the total, compared with 18 per cent in the Essex study (ONS, 2000b, table 4.11).

In 1998, there were about 40,000 children (26 per cent) aged less than five years in families of divorce, 68,000 (45 per cent) were aged 5–10 and 43,000 (28 per cent) were aged 11–15, inclusive (ONS, 2000a, p.46). The Essex study figures show a very similar age distribution for families of divorce but the corresponding proportions for families of cohabitation are strikingly different, as follows: 64 per cent of children were aged less than five years, 33 per cent were aged 5–10, and 3 per cent were aged 11–15. Families of cohabitation at mediation were therefore much more likely to involve younger children, nearly two thirds having been less than five years old. In combination with the high proportion of single children in such families, this might be interpreted as grounds for arguing that families of cohabitation are more likely to be 'simple', rather than 'complex', in terms of the opportunities for parental dispute and, as a result, by way of the number of 'problems' they might pose for mediators.

In 1996–1997, step-families, either remarried or cohabiting, accounted for around 8 per cent of all families with dependent children in Great Britain. In 84 per cent of step-families, at least one child was from a previous relationship of the woman and, in 12 per cent of step-families, there was at least one child from the man's prior relationship: in 4 per cent of step-families there were children from both. Surveys from the early 1990s suggest that perhaps 5.5 per cent of children aged under 16 years had experienced the separation of their natural parents and were living in step-families. Some children of divorce are subsequently raised by a lone parent, usually their mother, but it is possible that half will be brought up by their mother and the man she later marries. Within such 'new' families, further offspring may ensue and each year there are around 40,000 births to such remarriages. In 1991, it is estimated that about one million children were living in families that included one or more step-children (Cretney, 2000, p.9). Of course, many divorced parents go on to produce children within new partnerships of cohabitation, rather than marriage, for which similar figures are not readily available. Recent research has shown significant differences between disordered families of marriage and cohabitation, in terms of how quickly the resident parent is able to establish a new partnership. It is estimated that, on average, children spend 1.7 years with one parent, if their parents had been married, 4.3 years with one parent, if their parents had cohabited, and 6.6 years with one parent, if they had been born within a single parent household (Ermisch, 2000). Such findings may be interpreted as reflecting the differential experiences and opportunities of the three groups within a wider context of discrimination in favour of marriage (Bennett, 2000), although it is perhaps sufficient to say at this point in the writing that divorce is more likely to generate new two-parent households than is the dissolution of partnerships of cohabitation. As a result, it would be reasonable to suggest that mediation cases arising from divorce might be more likely to involve some consideration of 'new partners' and more likely to include the additional complications of 'new children', that is step- and half- siblings of the children to whom the mediation is devoted.

In summary, it is apparent that gauging the demand for mediation services will always be difficult, given the changes in social behaviour, affecting the numbers of disputes, and the interplay of a wide range of factors shaping the complexity of cases. Services that employ a series of meetings with couples and/or adopt a long-term therapeutic approach are likely to need a high level of resourcing, although cost would still have to be set alongside effectiveness in order to establish 'best value'. For county court mediation, normally comprising only one brief meeting between parents, their legal representatives and mediator(s), a highly complicated case may generate a significant level of additional tension and constitute a considerable increase in demand. Within the context of a busy schedule of meetings, even one such case may have important ramifications for mediator performance both in terms of outcome and in terms of process.

## A New Agency for Family Support Services

In bringing this introduction to a close, some mention of the arrival of the new unified agency, CAFCASS is clearly apposite. The immediate background to this development may be readily deciphered from the Department of Health *et al.* (1998) consultation paper, 'Support Services in Family Proceedings: Future Organisation of Court Welfare Services'. The consultation period ended in November 1998 and was speedily followed by an announcement from the Lord Chancellor that a new, non-departmental public body, the Children and Family Court Advisory Service, would be set up to combine the three existing services, that is the Guardian *ad Litem* and Reporting Officer (GALRO) Panels, the Family Court Welfare Service – an arm of the probation service – and the Children's Branch of the Official Solicitor's Department. The subsequent expansion of the name of the agency in 2000, so as to more accurately reflect its advisory and support brief, produced the acronym 'CAFCASS'.

A Project Team, under the directorship of David Lye, Department of Health, and including a representative from the Home Office, was given the following brief:

> To establish a high quality and cost effective unified Children and Family Court Advisory Service for England and Wales within a statutory framework and an agreed timescale,
> * Maintaining standards and minimising disruption in the delivery of existing court welfare services in the period of transition
> * Within an agreed budgetary framework
> * Establishing measurable national quality standards for a new service
> * Maximising commitment of service members and stakeholders
> (Lord Chancellor's Department, 1999).

A Project Development Group was also set up, with terms of reference to assist the Project Team, by advising on the development of proposals to establish CAFCASS, and to help secure the commitment of staff groups within the three constituent bodies to the new unified agency. The Group first met in September 1999 with a membership including representatives from the Association of Chief Officers of Probation, Central Probation Council, National Association of Probation Officers, Association of Family Court Welfare Officers, Her Majesty's Inspectors of Probation, Official Solicitor's Department, National Association of Guardians *ad Litem* and Reporting Officers, Association of Panel Managers, Local Government Association, Association of Directors of Social Services, Justices' Clerks' Society, The Court Service and the National Assembly for Wales.

The requirements for the new agency to be covered by primary and subordinate legislation, and transitional powers, were outlined in chapter six of the aforementioned consultation paper (Department of Health, 1998). The Criminal Justice and Court Services Bill presently going through Parliament is expected to gain Royal Assent in April 2001 and will act as the primary legislation necessary for transfer of assets and the like. Family Court Welfare accommodation, for example, will be transferred to the Home Office as part of the Probation Estate, before subsequent transfer to CAFCASS.

In addition to the many strategic and logistical matters certain to face CAFCASS, a set of issues stemming from the impact of the *Human Rights Act, 1998* looks likely to require attention. Article 12 establishes a right to marry without the intention to procreate but there is no right to found a family outside marriage. Protection for unmarried couples with children must be sought under Article 8 of the Act, the 'right to respect for private and family life'. Article 8 imposes obligations on the State not to interfere with individuals and to protect individuals against interference. The existence of 'family life', within the meaning defined by the European Convention of the Protection of Human Rights and Fundamental Freedoms, may be argued on the basis of fact and degree, even outside marriage: the fact that cohabitation occurred and the persistence and stability of the relationships therein may therefore be regarded as defining features of family life. To date, the European Court has adopted a rather narrow interpretation of 'family', so as to exclude homosexual relationships, but it may be that a broader reading will occur in the future. Whatever, it is widely acknowledged that the *Human Rights Act* may have implications for contact issues and hence for the resolution of disputes. Furthermore, articles other than 8 and 12 may have relevance: Article 14, for example, that proscribes discrimination on grounds of sex, race, language etceteras, has an evidently wide pertinence (Cretney, 2000, pp.14–15). In addition to the possible effects of the *Human Rights Act*, the government has recognised the implications for family courts of the emphasis placed by the international community on the representation of the child's viewpoint, as expressed in Article 12 of the United Nations Convention on the Rights of the Child. Although the Convention was ratified by the United Kingdom in 1991, there is an acceptance that further room for improvement exists within the realm of private law proceedings (Department of Health *et al.*, 1998, p.8).

The announcement by the Lord Chancellor on 17 June 1999 that implementation of Part II of the *Family Law Act 1996* was to be further delayed led to considerable trepidation about the future of UK mediation services (Nichols, 1999). As a consequence, attention on the new agency's pronouncements regarding mediation has been all the more intense. On the basis of statements made it is fair to conclude that, although there is no doubting the scale of change summoned by the creation of CAFCASS, it would be inaccurate to suggest that 'mediation', as presently understood, is likely to disappear. While recognising the wide variations in practice across England and Wales, CAFCASS has acknowledged the popularity of mediation with judges and there is a clear commitment from the agency to continue to fund mediation (CAFCASS, 2000, p.5). It is also apparent that the aims and functions of the new service will, at least initially, be almost identical to the preceding arrangements and, furthermore, it is apparent that the deliverers of front-line service are to be drawn from present staff groups. A review of professional accreditation and training is currently underway, although it is recognised that the vast majority of practitioners joining CAFCASS will have social work qualifications: the indications are that the present professional qualification, the Diploma in Social Work, is regarded as offering a suitable foundation for mediation practice. Working practices are, therefore, likely to be transferred and the 'new' mediation, as experienced by parents in dispute, may closely resemble its immediate forebears. With this in mind, the significance and timeliness of this book, and, indeed, the empirical study on which it is founded, are amplified, rather than detracted from, by the arrival of CAFCASS.

# 2    The Significance and Duration of Agreements Reached in Mediation

This chapter searches for a sense of the significance of mediation through reflections upon contemporary discourse and previous research, and via interpretations and analyses of data from the Essex study concerning the purposes, achievements and disappointments of mediation as experienced by parents. Various aims are proscribed by government for mediation: area services and individual family court officers work within this framework of expectation but are able to add their own emphases and predilections: parents come to mediation with a range of expectations of their own: and the very process and outcome(s) of the meeting may also be variously construed by the mediator(s), solicitors and parents involved. Given the span and depth of such complexities, it would be tempting then to call a halt, to contend that nothing more of worth might reasonably be said on the meaning and value of mediation – most sharply, that questions of overall effectiveness should remain unasked and unanswered. How effective is child-centred, county court mediation? How long do mediation agreements endure? What happens to them over time? When agreements do change, are parents pleased or unhappy about it? It would be tempting to relegate such questions to a second order of priority but the stance taken in this chapter is that these are perfectly legitimate enquiries, especially within a wider context of scarce resources and vigorously competing claims. This is not, of course, to suggest that prudence and circumspection are anything other than of central importance in the design and execution of evaluatory studies within this field.

Perhaps the most readily accessible measure of efficacy is the proportion of mediation meetings that end with an 'agreement'. Of course, this immediately begs questions of definition and perspective but nevertheless looks to be a useful and justifiable quantification. Annual statistics for individual mediators, teams, courts and areas may be assembled and compared with other family court services across the country. Similarly, agreement rates for 'child-centred' mediation may be compared with those from 'all issues' mediation and so on. Walker *et al.* (1994, p.71) argue that 'The purpose of mediation...is the resolution of disputes, hence the measure most commonly used to determine "success" has been the "settlement rate"'.

But what if all such settlements vanished within a few days of the mediation meeting? In such, admittedly extreme, circumstances what would 'settlement' actually mean? What could be its significance? As things stand at the moment, family court services offer and continue to deliver mediation without having access to research evidence on the duration of agreements reached: this is an uncomfortable position and one that cannot be easily consoled. In the broader climate of 'best value', a key part of the government's modernisation agenda for public services, the position, in fact, may barely be tenable. Without such and similar data, mediation services are unable to meet the need to evaluate their work and ill-equipped to compare and contrast their own efficacy with levels of success announced by their competitors.

**A Multitude of Aims**

Achieving a consensus on what 'success' or 'failure' might mean in the field of mediation would be relatively simple provided agreement could be reached on the aim(s) of mediation itself. In any individual case, gauging effectiveness would require nothing more than a comparison of aim and achievement. However, there are few such cases in the field of mediation and, indeed, in many other areas of professional practice. The reality is that many possible purposes exist for mediation overall and that, in any specific case, an 'eclectic' mix of aims may be present, although not always consciously acknowledged by all parties concerned. The government's proposals paper, *Looking to the Future: Mediation and the Ground for Divorce* (Lord Chancellor's Department, 1995), presents three primary objectives for family mediation:

- to help separating and divorcing couples to reach their own agreed joint decisions about future arrangements;
- to improve communications between them; and
- to help couples work together on the practical consequences of divorce with particular emphasis on their joint responsibilities to co-operate as parents in bringing up their children (para. 5.6).

However, the same document also states that family mediation can encourage couples to:

- seek marital counselling if it is appropriate to attempt to save the marriage;
- accept responsibility for the ending of the marriage;
- acknowledge that there may be conflict and hostility, and a strong desire to allege fault and attribute blame;
- deal with their feelings of hurt and anger;
- address issues which may impede their ability to negotiate settlements amicably, particularly the conduct of one spouse;
- focus on the needs of their children rather than on their own personal needs (para. 5.4).

The setting of such a lengthy list of objectives poses serious problems for the would-be evaluator. First, different mediators may select different aims for the same case and those aims might also be differently weighted or prioritised. Second, some parents will have a much clearer understanding than others of the objectives of their mediation session – such variations may arise from different levels of expectation and previous experiences of mediation, also from different mediator emphases to making goals explicit. Third, objectives may 'interact', in the sense that meeting one aim may affect the likelihood of meeting other aims. Finally, many of the objectives are constructed in a way that would make operationalisation very difficult to achieve. Needless to say, it would be much simpler if the number of aims was limited and if they could be set with measurement in mind.

Similar difficulties are to be found in other areas of professional endeavour in the social welfare sphere: Cheetham *et al.* (1992, p.16), for example, in the field of social work, write that:

The goals, processes and effects of social work are both diverse and difficult to capture in the terminology of standardized 'variables' that researchers commonly and necessarily employ...Any worthwhile research approach to effectiveness...is likely to have to live with various kinds of imprecision or elusiveness in some of its key terms,

and even in the, ostensibly, much more closely defined arena of sentencing practice within the criminal courts, it is possible for Brownlee (1998, p.165) to argue that '...the sentence which is chosen with one single, clear and carefully articulated objective in mind is a rarity...'.

Finally, it is important to acknowledge the limitations of measurement even in cases where the objective(s) can be stated with some certainty and precision. Discussions in this area are well rehearsed but there is value in highlighting the difficulties of progressing from an identified association between 'variables' to the establishment of a causal connection, in the social realm. So, it would be eminently reasonable to claim a statistically significant correlation between a defined outcome of mediation and, for arguments sake, the number of children in the family, but such a discovery would not mean that a causal ordering of the two variables could be legitimately assumed.

## What Works in Family Mediation?

It would be fair to say that the present level of knowledge and evidence on this question of efficacy in family mediation is far from adequate. The profusion and diversity of professional practice wisdom(s) conspire with the extant multiplicity of purposes at times to produce a virtually impenetrable discourse. It is possible, for example, to read Lindstein and Meteyard's (1996) tome, entitled *What Works in Family Mediation*, from cover to cover without encountering any acknowledgement that it might be helpful to know, roughly, what proportion of mediation meetings, or series of meetings employed in one case, result in settlement and how long the agreements might be expected to last. A host of potentially significant factors are discussed and related to individual cases, but the reader is left with no sense of how effectiveness might be gauged in overall terms. The power held by practitioners appears to be particularly strong in this domain and may be related to their association with the courts – and, in turn, to the ascendancy of a 'case-law' approach therein. Research by Parker *et al*. (1989) and Holdaway and Mantle (1992) describes a 'case-by-case' approach adopted by sentencers in the criminal courts that tends to find its way into policy-making processes, in which a much broader mode of thinking and decision-taking is required. There are grounds to suggest that, in the civil courts, decision-makers may also find it difficult to transcend a case-by-case mode of operation.

Davis (1998) opines that many of the principles that appear to guide practitioners have more to do with 'legal folk lore' (p.90) than with either research or legislation. This theme has been further developed by Davis and Pearce (1999) and subsequently by Jones (1999, p.255), who calls for a knowledge base for civil work founded upon research evidence and social science theory, in addition to practice wisdom, and cites the view of

Cantwell *et al.* (1998) that such a foundation would provide a useful counter to the current dominance of case law.

Research in this field also appears to have remained in the backwoods. Occasional efforts have been made to progress the debate but to little apparent effect. Hay *et al.* (1992, p.150), for example, offer the following account:

> The one performance indicator which the vast majority of court welfare officers might accept as indicating something of significance about their work is that of the rate of settlement of disputes. However, this makes major assumptions about the objectives of civil work which lie at the heart of much current practice...For example, is settlement seeking always a legitimate objective...? Can it only be achieved by family-focused approaches...? To what extent can the settlement be attributed to the court welfare officer as opposed to the vast array of other influences that can be exerted such as those that may emanate from other family members, friends or solicitors?

All of the points raised by Hay *et al.* are fair and apposite. However, neither individually nor collectively ought they to constitute a valid reason for calling off the search for measurement. Mediators in Essex, during the study period 1998–1999, achieved a settlement in about 70 per cent of the mediation meetings held and about half of these agreements 'survived' for a six months period – according to the parents concerned – while others did not remain intact. About one fifth of those that did not last broke down within one week. These are important findings. They are neither conclusive nor prescriptive, but they do serve to enhance the debate by provoking a new and vital set of questions, and the absence of comparable measures and findings in earlier research (Walker *et al.*, 1994; McCarthy and Walker, 1996) begins to look all the more difficult to commend. The two research reports (the Newcastle Study) referred to are entitled, respectively, 'Mediation: The Making and Remaking of Co-operative Relationships: An Evaluation of the Effectiveness of Comprehensive Mediation' and 'Evaluating the Longer Term Impact of Family Mediation'. With such an advertised emphasis on 'evaluation', how can the lack of any concern with the intactness or duration of agreements made at mediation be understood? If the answer is that the indicators 'intactness' and 'duration of agreement' are simply too crude as measures, then surely the logic of the argument would need to also be applied to the notion of 'agreement'. Put another way, if 'agreement' can stand as hard currency (and the Newcastle Study authors appear to say it can – Walker *et al.*,

1994, pp.71–84), why cannot 'intactness' and 'duration of agreement'? How is it that such a rapid devaluation can occur?

One important difficulty may arise from the possibility that one parent may say the agreement is no longer intact, while the other believes it is still intact. If this lack of confirming mutuality were to be anything but infrequent, then the two measures – intactness and duration – would be of little validity and, not surprisingly, researchers in this field would be loathe to entertain them. It is important, though, to spell out exactly why previous service user research has been unable to deal adequately with this issue and, in essence, the reason is twofold: first, some prior studies – for example, Morgan (1996) – have not been designed to identify individual respondents – the researchers would not then be able to compare the responses of both parents; and, second, previous surveys have achieved such low response rates that the number of 'paired replies' (that is, from both parents), has been much too small to allow proper analysis. Walker *et al.* (1994), for example, report a 21 per cent return rate for their initial survey of parents who had been through child-focused mediation (p.22). Because of sampling attrition, the follow up surveys produced even lower returns so that, by the third study, only 80 questionnaires were secured and, of these, only eight were paired replies. By contrast the Essex study produced 65 pairs from a total of 345 returns and this much higher proportion can be attributed to the higher return rate (48 per cent). (An easy way to understand the mathematics of this is to consider what would happen if you had a reply from one parent of each pair in the sample {a 50 per cent return} – every additional reply would then of necessity produce a paired reply). A high rate of paired replies allows the researcher to examine whether or not the two parties in each individual case agree – on the intactness and duration of the mediation settlement – and to extrapolate the findings on 'mutuality' back to the original sample and population.

Furthermore, the Essex study findings appear to be rather good, compared with those from earlier studies, and arguably deserving of bold announcement instead of bashful concealment. Research at the South East London Conciliation Bureau in Bromley by Davis and Roberts (1988) gives a success rate of 45 per cent while Walker *et al.* (1994), in their study of mediation services supported by National Family Mediation, report comparable rates of 19 per cent for child-focused and 39 per cent for comprehensive mediation (p.71). So, even if all of the Essex mediation settlements that did not last six months are discounted, the adjusted rate (c.35 per cent) remains considerably higher than the voluntary sector (NFM) figure. This finding would appear to release a rather large feline creature amongst the pigeons of traditional wisdom: to illustrate the point,

Home Office National Standards (1994) state that 'Research suggests that mediation is more effective away from court premises' (p.11). This is an unusual statement to discover within a declaration of standards by central government and, furthermore, it appears to be founded upon shaky ground. Very little research has ever been carried out in this field, at least in the UK, and the evidence, in fact, appears to stem from work described by Ogus *et al.* (1989) concerned with conciliation, the forerunner of mediation. It is also intriguing to discover that earlier research had found in favour of in-court conciliation. Davis (1983) cites a study made by the Inter-Departmental Committee on Conciliation (the Robinson Committee) that argued for conciliation to take place on court premises on the grounds that it would be more likely to result in agreements that were in accord with the children's interests (p.135). This earlier research had received a great deal of methodological criticism and been largely discredited, leading to the commissioning by government of further study by the Conciliation Project Unit at Newcastle University. This subsequent research, reported by Ogus *et al.* (1989), produced findings contrary to the Robinson Committee's work and it is possible to argue that these were attributed additional credibility precisely because they were contrary. From the historical record there is a sense of government being 'bounced' from one policy assertion to another and it is not unreasonable to conclude that the case for or against in-court mediation must remain open to further debate and await the arrival of a great deal more empirical evidence.

The effectiveness of mediation has been measured through the use of a variety of indicators. Parkinson (1997, p.321) lists these as:

- the number of cases referred to mediation;
- settlement rates, based on counting agreements reached in mediation;
- the durability of mediated settlements, measured over a period of time;
- consumer satisfaction with the process and agreements reached;
- evidence that mediation reduces hostility and bitterness in divorce;
- evidence that it helps participants to talk together, to resolve their problems;
- evidence that it increases co-operation between divorced parents over their children;
- its effectiveness in protecting children's needs and welfare in divorce;
- its impact on legal costs, legal aid applications and avoidance of litigation;
- legal advisers' views of the extent to which mediation benefited their clients;
- its potential for encouraging reconciliation and saving 'saveable' marriages.

although it is difficult to locate studies that focus upon the durability of settlements over time – Morgan (1996) is one exception – and there appears to be every reason to call for further empirical work on this indicator of effectiveness.

Most of the outcomes identified by Parkinson look to be 'time-dependent', in other words, their measurement is likely to produce variable results according to when it is carried out. For example, the effect of mediation on 'hostility and bitterness' will surely depend on how soon after mediation the 'effect' is gauged and, indeed, McCarthy and Walker (1996, p.5) report that, in the long term, levels of conflict between divorced parents are unaffected by mediation. Relatedly, earlier studies of the long-term impact of child-focused mediation suggest that its effects may be short-lived (Kelly, 1990; FCDRC, 1991).

Predicting success in the field of mediation is still very much in its infancy and the search for reliable predictors remains a key objective for further evaluatory research. Parkinson (1997, pp.348–9) refers to studies by Depner *et al.* (1994), Irving and Benjamin (1992) and Kelly and Duryee (1992) that demonstrate how high levels of marital discord need not prevent parents from reaching agreement in mediation. A review of mediation research in Canada by Irving and Benjamin (1995) suggests that there are a number of factors closely associated with outcome failure, including rigidity in expectations, family violence, high stress levels and where one party is rejecting while the other is unable to accept that the relationship has ended. Furthermore, expectations of success need to be related to what is known about the persistence and intensity of ongoing conflict between divorced and separated parents (Rodgers and Pryor, 1998, pp.41–2). Drawing on the Newcastle research, Dowling and Gorell-Barnes (2000, pp.15–16) suggest that for perhaps one quarter of divorcing families there is no possibility of 'agreement'. The authors sound a warning that expectations of collaboration between many sets of parents should be realistic, rather than linked to some ideal type of disordered family which

> ...may organise professionals' beliefs and place too great an emphasis on a co-operative future...Disruptive processes are likely to include difficulties in communication between parents who are no longer living together, as well as patterns of quarrelling and aggressive behaviour.

Finally, it may be possible to use the conceptual framework devised by Maccoby *et al.* (1990), as a means of gauging, in broad terms, the likelihood of successful outcomes in mediation. Attention has been paid in the literature, for example, to the difficulties of attempting to help resolve disputes between 'conflicted' parents. However, 'disengaged' parties are also likely to experience problems in mediation – coming face to face possibly after years of indirect communication, via the children, may be particularly uncomfortable – and this is an aspect of mediation practice that perhaps warrants further consideration in the literature.

## The Nature of Agreement in Mediation

Most settlements achieved at in-court, child-focused mediation arise from applications made for contact orders: applications for residence orders produce the next highest proportion and the remainder stem mainly from combinations of contact, residence, 'parental responsibility', 'specific issue' and 'prohibited steps' orders – all of which can be made by the court under s.8 of the *Children Act 1989*. In the Essex study the percentages are 59, 16 and 25 respectively. Mediated agreements are therefore mainly concerned with contact issues and the following three examples are presented in order to illustrate their form, similarities and differences:

> Staying contact, 10am on Saturday until 10am Sunday, alternate weekends...one week holiday 20.6.98 – 27.6.98;

> Contact in principle, alternate weekends Friday to Sunday...two weeks in the summer holidays. Visiting contact;

> Contact at contact centre on the first open date, to be for four sessions only as a trial.

As can be seen, arrangements may involve staying, visiting or both forms of contact: they may stipulate times for delivery and collection of children or this may be left for the parents to negotiate at a later date: arrangements may also include statements about where contact is to take place and whether it will be 'supervised'. Contact centres are also available in many areas of the country: they are run by voluntary organisations and offer a neutral, structured environment for non-resident parents and their children to meet.

Although child-focused mediation does not address financial matters that might be in dispute, such concerns may often be of great significance to one or both of the parties and are likely to have some bearing, at least, on the outcome of any agreement reached at mediation. In the Essex study there were many such examples, from women who resented having to allow or facilitate contact between their children and fathers who had not made the requisite maintenance payments:

> The mediator was not interested in what my ex- had been doing, whether he'd been paying up or not but to me this is the main part of it as I'm having to struggle like a paid help while he's having a good time with his new girlfriend and still wanting to see the kids when it suits him not me...

> They only listen more to the father, even though he has never paid one penny to clothe her etc...I feel he got it all his own way and he's still got his hands in his pocket and laughing at me underneath...

> No pay, no see!

and from a smaller number of men who saw 'being taken to court' as a financial weapon used by their ex-partners:

> I would like the matter of costs to be made an issue as well. In my case my ex-wife is on legal aid and I am not. When I first questioned her motives for going to court her reply was 'it won't cost me anything, only you'. I was therefore forced to spend a considerable amount of money, just for her to try and get an order which was basically what I was asking for in the first place. I know money should not be an issue but it must be realised that some parents are willing to use this to get back at a partner.

Earlier research in the field of child-focused mediation has also pointed to the high incidence of differences over a wider range of issues: Walker *et al.* (1994), for example, report that one in three of their 'couples' were in disagreement about either property or financial arrangements. There is a powerful argument, therefore, that to be successful mediation needs to cover 'all issues', rather than focus entirely upon questions of contact and residence and, overall, this may be perceived as setting a limit to the potential effectiveness of child-focused practice. One important counter to this line is that attempting to address a wide range of issues simply multiplies the chances of not reaching an agreement and, where an agreement is achieved, of something going wrong after mediation. Findings from the Newcastle study offer some support to both arguments: twice as many child-focused as comprehensive mediations resulted in 'all issues' being agreed while, on the other hand, nearly twice as many comprehensive as child-focused mediations ended with no issues being agreed (Walker *et al.* 1994, p.71). However, it is clear that financial conflicts may endure and develop over many years as life circumstances change and children progress through their primary, secondary and tertiary education and training. There is no doubting the sense of grievance that many women carry because of the burden of care they shoulder and the apparent attempts to avoid financial responsibility made by their ex-partners:

> Recently he gave up a good job and put most of his capital into buying a house with his girlfriend who is unemployed. The plan he says is to do it up and run a business from it but in the meantime he gives me nothing for the three kids. The CSA say they can't do a thing because he's not earning. Every time I ask him for some help, like over paying something towards the school trips for the older two, he creates merry hell and takes it out on them. So on paper he's got an excuse but really this is his way of trying to make life as difficult as he can for me.

**Agreements That Changed and Their Duration**

As already pointed out in this chapter, there is surprisingly little in the way of research evidence on what happens to mediation settlements over time and findings from the Essex study are all the more significant because of this fact. Fifty-two per cent of agreements were said still to be intact at the six months point after mediation and, of the cases in which arrangements were no longer intact, 21 per cent had lasted less than a week, a further 30 per cent lasted between one week and one month, 27 per cent between one and three months and the remaining 22 per cent had endured from three to six months. These figures match closely with findings from the smaller survey by Morgan (1996): 78 per cent of the Essex agreements that broke down did so before the three months point, compared with 79 per cent in the study undertaken in West Glamorgan by Morgan. These are significant results suggesting that, where mediated settlements do not last, about one half break down within one month and a further three in every ten fail to persist beyond three months. The finding that about one half persist at least to the six months point may be interpreted as good news for mediation services, given the brevity and financial cost of the intervention involved.

Statistical analysis of the Essex study data has pinpointed a small number of factors associated with the persistence of agreements made at mediation. In regard to the background characteristics of the sample, the sole variable with a strong correlation with 'intactness' ($p<0.005$) is the number of children involved – where there is more than one child, the chance of arrangements being intact at the six months point is considerably reduced. This finding is in line with common-sense expectations: the greater the number of children, the more chances there are for arrangements to change. Two further factors showed a significant association with durability. First, the age of the sole or eldest child (p<0.05), although the relationship is complex in that, for children aged 7 to 12 years inclusive, the likelihood of arrangements remaining intact is reduced while, for younger or older children, the risk is not so high. Second, the type of court order originally applied for – applications for contact orders (p<0.015), rather than residence or combinations of orders (some including contact issues), show the highest risk of breakdown. The reasons for these two associations are not quite so easy to grasp and require further study. However, it is possible to say that, in relation to the age of the child, it may be that younger children are more willing to fit in with arrangements made by their parents while, for children aged 13 and above, parents are more likely to gear their expectations to the child's wishes and, importantly, to their need for flexibility and peer contact. In regard to the type of order, family court practitioners have not been surprised by the research finding: they recognise the increased chance of problems occurring in settlements stemming from contact order applications, pointing out that 'prohibited steps', 'specific issue' and residence applications tend to be more straightforward and readily settled – in contrast, issues of contact are more complicated, long-standing and subject to change.

These are exciting findings and pave the way for further study on the longevity of mediated agreements. Furthermore, an important caveat for future research in this field has emerged from close analysis of the 'paired replies' in the Essex study. It is possible to say that the two parties in an individual case *are* likely to agree on whether or not the mediation settlement is or is not still intact at the six months point but, when the settlement is said to no longer be intact, it is much more likely that they will disagree over *when* the settlement actually broke down. This cautionary note may be especially valuable for future studies that do not achieve the high rate of paired replies (that is from both parents) secured in the Essex study.

## In What Ways do Mediation Agreements Change?

My ex-wife broke them all within a week. I have had to return to Court twice since then and expect to return before the year is out.

It would be completely unreasonable to expect settlements made at mediation to remain unchanged for a protracted period of time. Some degree of change is highly probable given the complexities and developments common to families and their relationships. On the other hand, it is likely that parents will not welcome the occurrence of too rapid and/or too extensive alterations to the agreement settlement achieved at mediation – after all, they will have gone to considerable trouble and expense in order to construct the agreement. An important avenue into the question of what significance is attributed by parents to the 'agreement' would hence appear to be whether or not any changes to it are welcomed or regretted. In the Essex study, the vast majority of participants had not welcomed the changes made (mainly to contact arrangements). A very small number of participants reported changes that had been construed as an improvement or as no less satisfactory than the original agreement but, overall, the picture is clear – changes to mediated settlements, at least over the initial six months period, are not looked upon favourably by parents.

In categorising the Essex study replies, it is possible to distinguish two main types: first, those parties who report a change in the arrangements agreed, with contact still maintained; and second, those who indicate a total cessation of contact, sometimes resulting in a return directly to court or to a further mediation session. With regard to the range of changes accompanied by a continuation of contact, there are examples of substantial and much less substantial alterations having taken place. There are replies which suggest a much more dramatic response to apparently minor failings to keep to arrangements (such as being late) than might be expected, evidence of the continuing acrimony between many parents and indicative, perhaps, of a tension between the 'spirit' and 'letter' of the agreement reached at mediation.

## Why do Agreements Change?

> Because the children's mother wishes the children not to see their Dad at all – she puts every possible obstacle in the way to obstruct reasonable contact. She offers the children more attractive options instead of arranging these for non-contact times. The mother persistently alienates the children and tries to control contact – i.e. by telling the children, if your Dad's only staying in the house you might as well stay at home...you're only going if he's taking you out!!

In addition to charting the ways in which settlements are likely to alter over time it is also important to consider the reasons given by service users for such changes. Where agreements are no longer intact, at the six months point after mediation, the reasons most frequently given by parents are (a) the other party refuses to allow contact or to keep to the detail of the arrangements made for allowing contact; (b) the other party, in exercising contact, does not keep to the agreed arrangements; (c) the other party does not exercise contact, usually without providing an explicit reason; and (d) the child refuses to comply with the arrangements or changes residence themself. From an analysis of the responses given by 'pairs' it is possible to say that, in many cases, the applicant's call for more 'flexibility' is perceived by the respondent as an 'inability or unwillingness to keep to the agreed arrangements'. It is also important to register the high incidence of 'blaming the other party' and, indeed, the levels of antagonism, suspicion and disregard apparent within replies to the question of why agreements are no longer intact, as graphically illustrated by the following two quotations from the Essex study:

> Because my ex-partner is a selfish bitch and changes things to suit herself...

> When you have an intransigent ex-wife who defies everything the court tells her to do. She just laughs at the court...she is a fraud, perjurer and devious liar. She has certainly fooled you lot!

The dilemma for parents and for mediators of, on the one hand, seeking some degree of flexibility (especially for older children and for cases involving more than one child), while, on the other hand, attempting to establish a relatively stable agreement looks to be significant. The former requires a broad spirit of co-operation while the latter is more narrowly concerned with keeping to the letter of agreement. Perhaps the key to solving the dilemma is 'good communication' between the two parties but it is clear that many parents have experienced a lengthy history of just the opposite and, in a context of ongoing conflict, the axis of flexibility – stability simply becomes a further source of discontent.

## Could Anything Else Have Been Done?

> From the outset the arrangements were interpreted differently by both sides. I feel it would have been better to have the arrangements written down at the time, in detail so that no-one could interpret them in a way to suit themselves.

Mediation may be distinguished from other meetings involving family court officers, such as 'directions appointments', which are not 'privileged'. In broad terms, a privileged meeting is one in which anything said by either party may only be reported to the court if both parties agree. Although this does not appear to preclude the taking of notes during mediation, in practice there is a general reticence about recording and the information leaflet for service users provided by Essex FCS says quite clearly that notes will not be taken by anyone present during the mediation meeting. As can be seen in the above words from a participant in the Essex study, this may have unfortunate ramifications. It would be difficult to imagine a case for not having a written record of the mediated settlement and, indeed, National Standards for Probation Service Family Court Welfare Work (Home Office, 1994, para. 3.8, p.12) offer the following precept:

> In those cases where agreement is reached, the court welfare officer should provide each party with a copy of the agreement to pass to their solicitor...

Nevertheless, the overwhelming majority of Essex study participants, who had felt that something more could have been done at mediation to ensure that the arrangements would remain intact, wanted a written statement of the agreement. Perhaps the most likely answer to this conundrum is that family court officers do not provide a record of the agreement because of the presence of legal representatives – who, it is assumed, will write down the details on behalf of their clients. There may be problems with this approach: first, it is conceivable that solicitors may interpret the details of the agreement in a partisan fashion or simply misstate the arrangements agreed; second, many solicitors may simply not know that mediators have such expectations; and, third, a significant proportion of parents are not legally represented (about one quarter in the Essex study).

A further, important theme is the 'need for something stronger' – usually a court order that, in some cases, had subsequently been sought and made. In other words, parents in this category were more concerned with the enforcement of any agreement, rather than the spirit of conciliation that it might have engendered – they wanted a more defined, authoritative intervention, as the following sentiments illustrate:

> For the terms of the order (*sic*) to be 'non-negotiable' and explained to each party quite clearly. For the terms of the order only to be changeable for a) a very good reason – say a family wedding – and b) only by written request 30

days before. I have made arrangements/ bought tickets etc...to be phoned 12 hours before the defined time to be told my daughters will not be coming because they are sleeping round a friends or gone to see their Nan – all of which I consider should be arranged in their non-contact time, or at least to consult me before arrangements are made...

There is an evident tension here between the need for some measure of flexibility in the ongoing implementation of mediation agreements and the desire to keep parties to task. The quotation also points up the added difficulties likely to ensue when children are of an age to make their own 'arrangements' and, indeed, some participants in the Essex study did suggest that the effectiveness of mediation might be enhanced by paying greater attention to the child's wishes, especially where the child is older:

They should have let my daughter of 14 years come and put her own views across and what she wanted to do about seeing her father.

Of the 757 children in the Essex study, one fifth were aged ten years or above, with approximately 6 per cent being teenagers, suggesting that the issue of how to attain and incorporate the child's wishes should receive close and urgent consideration by the new unified agency. It is difficult to imagine what meaning or significance 'agreement' might possess without knowing this essential part of the equation and yet it is clear that some settlements do break down precisely because the child's wishes are insufficiently solicited and/or heeded. Sometimes children do not want to have face-to-face or staying contact with their non-resident parent, as tellingly illustrated in the following words:

A previous mediator seemed intent on sharing out the children like cake, based on the father's rights rather than the children's needs or wishes. He could not deal with a case where the children did not like their father...

and, when this is apparent, greater consideration could perhaps be given to the use of alternative forms of contact such as by telephone, via computer and by letter. There is little doubt that the maintenance of links is of profound significance for children but there is also no self-evident reason why, at least in the short-term, this may not be achieved by such means.

## Mediation and Longer-Term Co-operation

Given the fragility of many agreements, there looks to be value in considering any longer-term effects that mediation might have. If it could be demonstrated, for example, that even settlements of relatively short duration had subsequent positive outcomes long-term then the case for mediation would be considerably advanced. Is it possible for mediation to spark a 'spirit' of co-operation that endures beyond, and regardless of, the demise of a particular settlement? There is evidence to suggest that such is rarely the case. Participants in the Essex study were asked if mediation had helped them reach new 'agreements' when the initial settlements had broken down. Three quarters replied 'no' to this question and, of this group, most explained their response in terms of the other parent's unreasonableness or related failings, upon which mediation had had no impact, for example:

> The other party appears mentally incapable of sticking to any arrangements.

> My ex-wife's attitude and vindictiveness has caused the present arrangements. I have tried every different approach but I'm afraid I have lost the respect of my children and I fear I will never get it back.

It would be difficult to imagine any scope for mediation to alleviate such perceived difficulties, certainly not within current levels of resourcing, and it is fair to conclude that, for many parents, levels of conflict are unlikely to be affected by mediation. The meaning of 'agreement' in such circumstances is clearly worthy of further consideration and it is important to call attention here to the concern, expressed by critics of mediation, that parents may often feel obliged or forced to 'agree', especially in cases involving 'domestic violence'. Hester and Radford (1996, pp.46–7) argue that:

> Our research in England found that the result was often 'coerced' agreements which were invariably unsafe for women, and often unsafe for the children as well. In Denmark there is less concern with a quick, cheap agreement to shared child care, and a more pragmatic focus on ensuring that the parents are able to work effectively together in relation to the child's welfare. Agreement between parents is the preferred outcome, but there is recognition that this is not always possible or even desirable.

The idea that agreement may not always be 'desirable' cuts sharply across much of the traditional thinking about mediation: it reminds us that contact between the child and the non-resident parent cannot be the only issue on the table and that family violence must also be closely considered. Clearly, the 'welfare of the child' relates to both issues, although the research by Hester and Radford would appear to suggest that, at least in England, greater weight has been given to the child's need for contact with the absent parent. The relationship between violence and mediation is explored in chapter 4 of this essay, while the question of contact is further examined in chapter 3.

## User Perspective and User Satisfaction

Userism and consumerism are, as yet, ill at ease in probation service discourse and evidence of an interest in the user or consumer perspective within the probation service is not easy to find (Mantle, 1999, pp.20–9), although Davies (1994) cites a number of small-scale studies. Relatedly, the need to consult service users in family court work has only fairly recently been acknowledged. There are extensive literatures in the related fields of social work and health. In social work, the study by Mayer and Timms (1970) is regarded as the first to address the user perspective and reviews by Rees and Wallace (1982) and Fisher (1983) chart the subsequent growth in interest shown by researchers through the decade. Later reviews are provided by Howe (1987), Sainsbury (1987), Cheetham *et al.* (1992) and Macdonald *et al.* (1992), who analyse 95 studies of social work effectiveness, of which 24 were 'client opinion studies'. Howe (1987) relates this development of interest in the user's view to a broader movement in the social sciences '...away from seeing people as objects in society to understanding them as individuals who have personal views of the world' (p.3), while Everitt *et al.* (1992) argue that user study is one of the emergent responses to the methodological and ethical limitations of social work research based on positivism, a view shared by Mayer and Timms (1970, pp.14–16) in their own account of the late arrival of consumerism in social work. Howe (1990) argues that, while the user perspective is important, there is a need to consider other viewpoints as well. He also calls for researchers to add 'social theory' to the client's view, in order to provide an understanding of the nature of social work and of the wider context. There is merit in this position, although the appeal for theory can equally apply to the practitioner perspective and, indeed, to the researcher's view. Furthermore, Howe appears to imply that 'theorising' is the exclusive province of researchers, or, at least, not something to be expected, as a rule, from service users. This is erroneous and unfair. The value of listening to the subjective meanings of users, in a non-pathologising way, perhaps deserves some reinforcement.

Consumerism is an established theme in health service literature, a profile boosted by the *Patient's Charter* (Department of Health, 1991), and the public's opinion of the National Health Service is surveyed annually by the National Association of Health Authorities and Trusts – a review of these and other surveys is provided by Judge and Soloman (1993). There is a general acceptance of the need to ascertain the patient's level of satisfaction with the health service received and this is usually expressed in terms of 'quality assurance' (Green and Lewis, 1986; Koch, 1992). The arrival of 'community care' has served to cut across the health – social services divide and placed a new emphasis on the involvement of users and carers in service planning while the theme of 'exclusion' of particular groups from society appears in much of the literature of community care. These are major developments, shaping the way in which the relationship between service deliverers and consumers is construed, and it is necessary to locate family court mediation within this wider context of change and development. It is now much more difficult, for example, for family court services to resist suggestions that they might be more sensitive to user perspectives in their policies and practices.

The level of user satisfaction with a service is widely accepted as a key effectiveness outcome (Cheetham *et al.* 1992), although this is not to suggest that its measurement is ever straightforward or uncontentious and the inclination of users to report being 'generally satisfied' while bearing specific discontents is well-documented:

> It is therefore essential, we would argue, that the user perspective is sought through research instruments and methodologies sufficiently sensitive to counteract this tendency to broad statements of compliance (Fuller and Petch, 1995, p.42).

A more exhaustive account of the relevant findings from the Essex study is provided in chapter 6, so it is sufficient here to report that 70 per cent of participants had felt that their mediation session had been of an acceptable, or better, standard while 30 per cent had been dissatisfied or very dissatisfied. Of general interest to researchers in this field is the close association between the level of satisfaction and whether or not the agreed arrangements are still in place at the time when the 'satisfaction question' is asked. Although the Essex study research referred specifically to the mediation meeting, rather than with the process more generally, it is likely that some parents did not make the distinction between process and outcome and, therefore, that their responses could vary markedly depending on how long after the mediation event the question was put to them.

User expectations are often low and this is a significant consideration for evaluatory studies that incorporate a user or consumer dimension. Some three quarters of the Essex study participants had no particular expectations of mediation based on previous experience or knowledge, while those who had expectations referred to previous mediation meetings as their source of information. Most replies in this category indicated low expectations of the session: this might be predicted on the basis that prior attempts at mediation had evidently been unsuccessful, either in terms of reaching agreement or in terms of maintaining any agreement made:

> After three previous mediation meetings I had no belief that anything would come of it and was proved right. The past history was omitted. She has brought court cases many times wasting everyone's time. She will not make any commitment to the children...

> I was dreading it. I had been through two private mediation sessions and come out crying.

For those parents with no prior experience, the demands of the mediation session may come as a fairly sharp surprise and little comfort or preparation appears to be drawn from the information leaflets made available by family court services. Although it is apparent that solicitors do provide a valuable role in this regard, a preliminary meeting to discuss the purpose and parameters of mediation might nevertheless be usefully considered.

**Conclusion**

The reconstruction of mediation must involve a much closer awareness of and sensitivity to the views, theories and understandings of service users. The ascendancy of practitioner wisdom and of governance policies based on case law is ripe for review. Relatedly, it is not unreasonable to say that, to date, many researchers in this field have founded their work on an over-ambitious view of mediation. Walker *et al.* (1994), for example, talk in terms of 'making and remaking co-operative relationships' which, for many sets of parents is not a realistic ambition and there may be a danger that, in accepting such a demanding goal, more modest, measurable options may be afforded insufficient attention and worth. There is a need, therefore, to devise a different set of key targets and related yardsticks for mediation and the discussions within this chapter have demonstrated the potential value of using the 'intactness' of the agreement made at mediation as a measure of effective outcome. Such 'agreements' are important to many service users and, although they may fall far short of the ideal parent-to-parent relationship, in which a 'spirit' of co-operation transcends the more mundane realities of conflicting interest, their significance deserves more widespread recognition. Achieving an agreed set of arrangements is possible even when the intensity and history of discord mean that the parental relationship is unlikely to be 'co-operative' in a wider sense. The finding that parents normally concur as to whether or not their settlement is intact after a period of six months offers considerable support to the further employment of the 'durability of the settlement' as a valid and reliable indicator of performance.

The desire to reach an agreement, although important, cannot be the sole consideration for mediators and the issue of family violence deserves to be afforded similar attention. Women who have been abused should not feel obliged to attend mediation nor to reach 'agreement' with their ex-partners. However, although it would be difficult to imagine a convincing argument in favour of coercion, neither is it possible to contend that all mediated agreements must be entirely voluntary. Some shifting of position and a level of sacrifice by both parties must be involved in order to reach a settlement given the inevitable conflicts of interest involved. 'Agreement' in this context therefore signifies mutual concession, negotiation and a relatively short-term programme of child care arrangements.

Just as the gauging of effectiveness can be a risky business, there are dangers too in the wholesale avoidance of measurement. Perhaps the most worrying is the reduction of 'best value' to 'lowest cost': in other words, if no additional indicators can be agreed upon – because of an ideological fixation with the sanctity of the individual case – then the sole remaining measurable is 'cost per mediation'. It would be both unfortunate and ironical if this were to happen especially in the light of the results of the empirical research undertaken in Essex. The finding that about one half of mediation agreements remain intact for at least six months is an important one. It suggests that this form of professional intervention can be a very effective means of assisting divorced and separated parents to manage their interactions regarding their children. The mediation event lasts an hour or so, a brief interlude, and yet holds significant gravity, purpose and efficacy for many parents who make use of it. On the issue of 'gravity', it is reasonable to argue that in-court mediation may have an advantage. The formality of the court may grant a useful weight, as well as a less helpful 'tension' to mediation proceedings. After all, many Essex parents who were critical of mediation expressed a desire for a more authoritative form of intervention and it is possible that the additional gravity and sense of occasion contributes to the likelihood of a successful outcome, albeit in a not too straightforward way – some parties may be swayed to make agreements that they do not really accept and these are less likely to stand the test of time; others will afford their agreement extra significance because of the court context and such agreements may be more robust over time.

The three indicators of success – settlement rate, intactness of agreement and user satisfaction rating – would appear to be the most appropriate, in conjunction with a suitable measure of cost. In regard to the appraisal of mediation, the issue of timing appears to be crucial and there is now firm evidence to suggest that the effects of mediation may be relatively short-lived which indicates that priority in evaluatory research might best be given to gauging effectiveness in the year or so after mediation has taken place. Furthermore, most settlements that fail to last actually break down within the first three months after the mediation meeting, a finding of enormous significance for researchers, practitioners and policy-makers alike. A strong case could readily be made for the implementation of some form of automatic follow-up or review by mediators of the settlements made.

Mediation is a grossly under-researched field and it is apparent that major policy commitments have been grounded on minimal and questionable evidence. Looking back over the decade, it is fair to cite the Newcastle Study as a major piece of influential research and, although it possesses many fine qualities, there are also a number of significant concerns about the work. Of special note are the low response rates for the surveys of parents (26 per cent for comprehensive and 21 per cent for child-focused mediation – Walker *et al*. 1994, pp.22–3) and the absence of any follow-up study on the durability of mediation agreements. With such shortcomings in mind, the currently accepted wisdom that in-court provision is inferior to out-of-court mediation looks to be in urgent need of review but there are many other areas of practice that also require further research. The involvement of children in mediation, for example, continues to be the subject of heated debate: Robinson (1999, p.140) is able to contend that 'Although little formal evaluation exists, children are increasingly involved in family mediation and this appears to be mainly beneficial…' while Dowling and Gorrell-Barnes (2000, p.186) take the view that 'From our own experience, we would suggest that children become a complicating factor in a mediation process'.

The common denominator for these two opposing positions is that they are both founded upon inadequate evidence and this chapter ends with a plea for a comprehensive programme of extensive, longitudinal studies to accompany the launch and development of the new unified agency. The reconstruction of mediation calls for firmer foundations of both theory and empirical evidence.

# 3    Fathers and Fairness

I was treated unfairly for one simple reason – because I am male. Had I been of the opposite gender, this would NEVER [original emphasis] have happened...one woman is allowed to take the children away from their whole family and the so-called experts just sit there and smile.

The notion of fatherhood has received a great deal of academic, public policy and lay attention during the past couple of decades (Lewis and O'Brien, 1987; Moss, 1995; Parke, 1996; Burghes *et al.*, 1997; Lupton and Barclay, 1997). Various constructions have been espoused and critically examined, while 'traditional' fathering has come to be seen, in most quarters, as distinctly unworthy, and the need for fatherhood to be reassessed, renegotiated or reinvented widely accepted (Gould and Gunther, 1993; Burgess and Ruxton, 1996; Burgess, 1997; Howarth, 1997). More recently, 'new' notions of fatherhood have begun to emerge, coincident with a contention that fathers can and do play important, 'generative' roles with their children (Hawkins and Dollahite, 1997; Dienhart, 1998). On a broader canvas, masculinity has itself been subject to exacting and protracted scrutiny (Pringle, 1995; Lloyd, 1996; Mac an Ghaill, 1996; Popay *et al.*, 1998), with significant debate around how men should and could 'change' (May *et al.*, 1996), and whether or not masculinities are changing fast enough (Segal, 1997).

In the context of child development, it is possible to identify relevant fathering literature concerned with infants (Lamb, 1997), pre-school and school-age children (Biller and Kimpton, 1997; Lewis, 1997) and adolescents (Hosley and Montemayor, 1997; Shulman and Seiffge-Krenke, 1997). There are works that focus on the relationships between fathers and their daughters (Sharpe, 1994) and on particular aspects of child welfare – for example, the child's mental health (Phares, 1998). Specific attention has also been paid to 'young' fathers and child development (Marsiglio and Cohan, 1997; Speake *et al.*, 1997). Cultural aspects of fathering have been addressed by Bozett and Hanson (1991) and there is a small, yet vital, American literature offering black perspectives on fatherhood (Barrow, 1996; Allen and Connor, 1997).

In terms of discourse, renditions of 'fatherhood' appear in the media, in 'expert' accounts – by psychologists, social workers and family therapists – in academic, social theorising (Lupton and Barclay, 1997, pp.8–34) and in autobiographical works. Not surprisingly, sharp differences in position and politics are readily apparent within and between each of these four categories. For the purposes of this book, it is perhaps sufficient to highlight discourses that construe fathering as being of some value in 'intact' families (Walker, 1996, pp.47–60) and discourses that, apparently, do not (Smart, 1999).

The literature concerned with single parent families is vast (Dennis, 1993; Donnellan, 1993; Kissman and Allen, 1993) and, because most single parents are women, 'fatherlessness' has also been afforded a great deal of attention by researchers and theorists (Daniels, 1998; Bradshaw, 1999). The significance of fatherlessness is keenly contested, with much depending upon how important fathers are perceived to be within intact families. Even where there is agreement that children may be disadvantaged by parental separation or divorce, there is no consensus as to the mechanism involved – impoverishment of the mother or lack of fathering is one key axis of disagreement in this debate. Finally, the position and experiences of fathers within the context of divorce have also been considered in the literature (Arendell, 1995).

A comprehensive review of research concerned with the outcomes for children of divorce and separation is provided by Rodgers and Pryor (1998), who write (p.15):

> After separation, children no longer live with one of their parents and often lose contact with kin associated with their non-residential parent... Numerous studies have documented the distress experienced by children and their families in these circumstances.

The progressive loss of contact over time between children and the non-resident parent, usually the father, has been recognised in the literature (Seltzer, 1991, Cockett and Tripp, 1994), as has the desire of children to maintain contact in such circumstances (Rodgers and Pryor, 1998, p.17). However, the relationship between contact and child adjustment is far from simple, with some studies reporting neutral or even negative effects of high levels of contact on the child's well-being (Furstenberg *et al.*, 1987; Baydar, 1988). Conflict between parents is likely to be a significant intermediary factor, as is the child's age, with teenage children opting for more 'flexible' arrangements.

There is a relatively sparse literature concerned with fathering after divorce (Lund, 1987, Kruk, 1989, Simpson *et al.*, 1995; Walker, 1996; Smart, 1999) within the wider arena of maintaining links between separated family members. Bradshaw and Miller (1991) found that, in their study, about four out of every ten fathers did not stay in contact with their children after divorce, although there is evidence that this state of affairs may be changing (Brown, 1994; and Walker, 1996 – who found that more than 60 per cent of fathers saw their children at least once a month) and indications that patterns of contact may vary significantly from country to country – Gibson (1992) reports an Australian research finding that about two thirds of children had face-to-face contact with their fathers, at least fortnightly, two to five years after separation.

There is a long-standing assumption in the UK and, indeed, in many other countries that contact with both parents is always the preferred option in regard to promoting and safeguarding the welfare interests of the child. Since the *Children Act 1989*, this assumption has been afforded full legal recognition with both parents, after divorce, retaining the responsibility they had when married. The paramountcy of contact, even in families where the father has been abusive to mother and/or children, is a key feature of professional and legal discourse and there is evidence to suggest that the emphasis given to contact, over, for example, the issue of the child's safety, is greater in the UK. Hester and Radford (1996, p.46), on the basis of their comparative study in England and Denmark, report that:

> Where mothers disagreed with their ex-partners about contact due to concerns about safety, their concerns were more likely to be taken into account by Danish professionals. Lack of agreement would be seen as indicative of problems for any future arrangements for the children.

Establishing and maintaining contact between children and their non-resident parent, usually the father, is thus a key objective for all those concerned with family court policy and practice. However, there is little in the legislation to indicate the purpose of such linkage, of the 'role' to be played or the nature of the fathering to be delivered. In effect, the father is granted a 'right' to contact, with no guidance nor expectation as to what such contact might involve or contribute towards. Put sharply, is the purpose of contact, simply, to maintain a relationship into the child's adulthood or is the aim to allow fathers an opportunity to play an active and crucial part in the child's up-bringing? This debate may then be set in the context of different views on what fathers do, and the significance of

what they do, in intact families. If fathers generally act as providers and
have less important, affective bonds with their children, than do mothers,
then, after divorce, should a similar pattern prevail or might fathers need
or want to change their approach? Smart (1999), who views the question
from a position that construes fathering, pre-separation, as being of little
value aside from financial maintenance, concludes that (1) fathers who
insist on contact without changing their approach – in terms of accepting
more responsibility for carework – are likely to cause difficulties and
strains within the family; and (2) fathers are ill-equipped to make such
adaptation. Smart (1999, pp.112-13) develops a powerful account of how
mothers are subject to socio-economic disadvantage in the struggle to
adjust:

> Entry into post-divorce family life therefore poses problems. For the father
> they reside in the problem of forming a direct relationship with children and
> winning the support of his former wife to do this. His problems are
> substantial. He does, however, have the full support of the Children Act, the
> legal profession and the mediation service if he decides on this course of
> action. With luck he will also have the support of his own mother and a new
> partner who can ensure that his enhanced fathering role does not interfere
> with his role as independent wage-earning citizen. For the mother the
> problems are of a different order. She must give up her 'special'
> relationship (for the sake of the children) and hence her status as a primary
> carer. But she must also amend her status as a dependant, earn enough
> money to support herself and (in part) the children, accrue benefits against
> the exigencies of illness and old age, and become autonomous, self-
> sufficient and self-confident…In this process she is unlikely to have much
> support from the Children Act, the legal profession or the mediation
> services, none of whom give priority to, or even much consideration to, the
> needs of mothers.

added to which might be the difficulties experienced by women with
children in forming new adult relationships and, in summary, it is
reasonable to suggest that mothers face a much more difficult set of
challenges than do fathers when unions dissolve.

In response to Smart's analyses, it is possible to contend that much
of her argument's momentum depends upon a 'deficit' model – i.e. that it
ignores the many examples of 'good' fathering – and that it runs the risk of
discouraging the development of more involved, caring patterns of
relationship between fathers and their children. Furthermore, the case of
(resident) fathers who act as primary caregivers is apparently ignored and,
finally, the research findings that 'new' fathers express both a sensitivity

to the failings of their own fathers and a desire to be much more involved with their children is not addressed. Lupton and Barclay (1997, p.121) review Canadian and Australian studies that suggest a new fatherhood, at least in terms of ambition:

> Daly (1993) found that the men tended to compare themselves against their own fathers as points of reference for how they were 'different', rather than using their fathers as a positive role model...White (1994) found that all the men described their fathers as having little involvement with them when they were children and talked about the 'lack of closeness' in their relationship with their father. They often positioned themselves as attempting to achieve a different and 'better' relationship with their own children.

Rather than presenting fathers as lacking the will to change, some writers have invoked a celebratory portrayal designed to encourage transformation (Hawkins and Dollahite, 1997, p.15):

> Because the RIP (Role-Inadequacy Perspective) gives little attention to the processes of men's adult development, it fails to locate parenting at the center of men's lives, which is where many fathers put it and where most fathers know it must be.

Hawkins and Dollahite offer no empirical evidence for their assertions concerning what fathers do and what they know but, on the other hand, it would be difficult to contest the view that some examples of good fathering exist. It is also fair to say that many obstacles exist to the exercise of constructive fatherhood, especially when couples separate and divorce. Finally, Blankenhorn (1995) points out that society offers little if any guidance on how to be a good father in such circumstances and some writers have linked the absence of cultural norms for separated parenting to the move towards individualism that has allowed men to develop their own modes of fathering, however irresponsible and neglectful such adaptations might be (Doherty, 1997).

In summary, there are two major perspectives on fatherhood – one that fathers are unnecessary or deficient, and the other that fathers are (successfully) struggling to provide something positive, in the face of social barriers. For the purposes of this essay, it is sufficient to present these two, contrary positions – Smart, on the one hand, and Hawkins and Dollahite, on the other – as helpful conceptual resources in the development of an appropriately rounded account of fathers and mediation. It is against this discursive backcloth that questions of 'fairness' in post-divorce negotiations and settlements need to be set.

## Mediation and Fathers

The concept of 'neutrality' is particularly helpful in exploring the meaning and perplexities of family mediation. There are two crucial senses in which the word might be employed: first, as a way of signifying that the mediator should remain unbiased, fair or even-handed in their practice with individual sets of divorced parents; and second, that, in more broad terms, the mediator should avoid any challenges to the *status quo* – i.e. the prevailing views and legitimacies on parenting. Both usages readily provoke important debates and it is quickly apparent that two major dilemmas underlie mediation work – in question form, how can mediators remain 'fair' in their day-to-day practice without taking into account wider inequalities of power, especially in terms of gender, and how should practitioners respond to social changes, especially the, albeit contested, emergence of 'new' fatherhood?

Not surprisingly, the relevance of both debates is immediately apparent in the commentaries of parents who have undergone mediation. When parents in the Essex study were asked if they had ever been treated unfairly during mediation, only 16 per cent replied in the affirmative and, of these, the vast majority of replies were concerned with the issue of gender. For men, there was a sense of having been discriminated against because of social assumptions about the relative importance of fathers and mothers to their children, 'I felt that my gender was an issue during mediation. I felt that as a man I was regarded as unimportant in my children's well-being', whereas, for women, the sense of unfairness related to the 'burden of care':

> I would like my money back! I am broke, bringing up 2 children alone whilst my husband is shacked up with a girl...driving around, having his cake and eating it. I think mediators should be aware of the situation and maybe weigh the scales a little...

and to a lack of sensitivity to the issue of domestic violence (see chapter 4). Women also referred to a reluctance on the part of fathers to 'put themselves out', 'My ex-husband refused to take time off work or include children in his holiday time', resulting in a reduction in contact even though the father's original application to the Court had been for an opportunity to see more of his children:

> They visited him in the school holidays but only for two days...nothing has been done to make him keep to the arrangements and the children are disappointed that what was arranged has not been kept to.

In this case, the father made reference both to difficulties in taking time off work, a resonance of the concerns and confines of 'old' fatherhood, and to his desire to spend time with his new partner. The impact of new relationships, for non-resident fathers and, less frequently, for resident mothers, was evident in a number of testimonies.

> Because part of the arrangement was that the children did not associate with my husband's current partner, he decided that it was too 'awkward' for him to see them at weekends, so he only sees them for two hours per week after school.

In regard to fathers' ideas of 'fairness', Walker *et al.* (1994, p.79) highlight the fact that many fathers agree to mediation settlements because they believe that what they are offered, in terms of contact, is all they are likely to receive. In other words, they are obliged to limit their aspirations in the face of what is deemed reasonable by mediators, solicitors and the courts more widely – they may therefore leave mediation with a settlement that they would acknowledge as 'fair', by the benchmark of tradition or precedent, but may also have a deeper sense of unfairness in terms of their own desires. Mediators may thus be adjudged as fair but only as neutral purveyors of accepted wisdom and, for this, they are open to trenchant challenge. Wilding (1982, pp.99–103), for example, in his celebrated critique of professional power, unpicks the claim for 'neutrality' advanced by social welfare professionals to reveal an inherently political stance devoted to conservatism – the unquestioning reproduction of one (unquestioning) version of the past. Lipsky (1980) observes the tendency for professionals, in the face of heavy workloads combined with the stress of working directly with members of the public, to adopt bureaucratic modes of practice. In the mediation context, where practitioners do face onerous demands, it would not be surprising to locate such a proclivity to employ 'standardised' ways of assessment and intervention and, indeed, the Essex study data provides many pertinent examples.

> From when it started I thought that it was already stitched up. The mediator had it in his mind what was going to happen and there was no way he was going to listen to anything different. I think they should be more open minded, not that everyone can be fitted in to one way.

Again, this points to an in-built preference for the *status quo*: challenging it is likely to prompt a reaction from other powerful stakeholders who will expect a 'justification' for the unusual. An individual father's sense of fairness needs to be examined against this backcloth of insights drawn from organisational studies and it is reasonable to suggest that 'new' fathers are likely to face an uphill struggle. Those men with a greater awareness of the debate around, and politics of, new fatherhood may experience particular unease, as illustrated in the following words from a father who had decided on a strategy of direct confrontation with the upholders of traditional practice.

> In spite of the fact that, when I challenged each person I came into contact with that the legal system is always biased against the male parent in cases of custody, all began by saying that this was not so, anybody who did not have the power to simply overrule me was eventually forced to agree that in fact it was so. It is notable that those with magisterial power did overrule me usually with a threat of removal from court. The 'arbitrator' had no such power but she did make reference to the likelihood that unless I 'agreed' to my ex-wife's proposition a judge would enforce it – neatly closing the circle.

This testimony is most untypical and there is little in the Essex study data to suggest the emergence of a significant number of highly politicised, new fathers. Nevertheless, the example does serve to point up the sense of frustration that many fathers experience and it would not be unreasonable to argue that, without some feeling of access to a broader political sensitivity and organised 'movement', individual fathers may develop a profound sense of inadequacy and disempowerment.

## The Gender of the Mediator

The gender of the mediator (or genders if more than one mediator is involved) is evidently of interest in discussions of perceived fairness, although many writers in the field of mediation have apparently afforded little, and sometimes no, significance to the issue (Haynes, 1993; Lindstein and Meteyard, 1996). In common with other studies, findings from the Essex study suggest that, overall, service users do not consider gender to be a significant issue: 91 per cent of parents answered that the mediator's gender had not mattered (the comparable figure is 81 per cent in Morgan's, 1996, study). Most fathers had apparently not been concerned with whether the mediator was male or female. Nevertheless, a small but significant minority would have preferred a male mediator to have been present on the grounds that a male would not have been as 'biased against fathers'. This is an especially interesting finding because it marks a strong contrast with previous studies and may signify one of the first effects of a growing politicisation of fathers, on the heels of the growing influence of pressure groups such as 'Families Need Fathers' and 'Fathers Direct'.

The picture for mothers is more complex in that some Essex study participants wanted a female mediator, because of an expected greater sensitivity, for example 'A woman that had had children could see more of a child's view...I felt she was very understanding', while, as discussed further in chapter 4, other mothers perceived a male mediator as an important provider of protection from their aggressive ex-spouse:

> It's proven men are stronger than women, yes it's good women are there but the men were too elderly to intervene if my children's dad were to attack me again.

Once again, these findings from the Essex study reinforce those from earlier works: Walker *et al.* (1994, p.128) reports that one mother in the Newcastle study made a similar plea for a male mediator:

> Some ex-husbands do not respond to women conciliators. He often tried to control the sessions and talked down to women conciliators.

The benefits of co-mediation – having more than one mediator present – are well-documented (Parkinson, 1997, pp.339–40) and it is important to recognise that the question of gender assumes a heightened significance when two mediators are involved. Previous studies have shown that, when two mediators of the same sex are present, both male and female parents can feel 'outnumbered' or even intimidated and there is some empirical evidence to support the view that a mediator of each gender can produce fairer agreements (Adler and Barnes, 1983), although there is little doubt that a great deal more research is required in this area. Morgan (1996) reports that only 52 per cent of parents in her study said that gender would not matter in co-mediation cases, compared with 81 per cent when only one mediator had been present.

One Essex study father had felt especially 'alone' because the mediator and both solicitors were female,

> I was the only male in a room full of females and I felt that the maternal issue was better understood and indeed commented upon even though I, as the father, had and have been more close and responsible to my children...Just a niggly feeling of womanhood, we feel something you don't feel kind of thing...I think there should be two mediators, one of each sex,

and the danger that such circumstances will leave one parent with a profound sense of unfairness needs to be carefully considered by mediators, by those responsible for their management and by legal representatives. It is worth noting that a similar call, albeit in respect of both mediators being the same sex, had been made more than a decade ago by researchers based at the Conciliation Project Unit (CPU, 1989).

The notion of an advantageous 'balance' associated with having two mediators, one of each gender, is readily understood and often appears in the mediation literature (Parkinson, 1997, pp.72–3). The temptation to see such an arrangement as inevitably more 'fair' is hard to resist but the following words from an Essex study mother provide an illuminating, alternative view, 'a woman mediating for me and a male mediating for him I feel didn't help matters as it ended up sexist', that alerts us to the fact that fairness may have a number of different, possibly contradictory, meanings and also sirens the danger of a drift towards an adversarial form of engagement. In a court setting, with solicitors present, the risk may be all the greater, a question that is explored in chapter 5.

Mediators need to be aware of the risks of 'lining up' with the same sex parent and to take careful stock of the impact of solicitors on the gender aspects of the mediation meeting. Of course, this precept needs to be taken alongside a more general call for co-practitioners to be aware of, and take action to redress, the power imbalances between parents, especially those related to gender, that are frequently apparent at mediation and there may therefore be difficult tensions for mediators to face. On the one hand, co-mediators will want to avoid any suggestion of 'women versus men' while, on the other hand, they will also want to ensure that mothers are not dominated by their ex-partners. This is an issue that has, to date, not been sufficiently addressed in the mediation literature and might readily form the centre of a research study into how co-mediators manage such dilemmas. In terms of theory, the tension provides an important invitation to review notions of 'fairness' within a range of professional practice contexts – at one end of the spectrum might be posited an 'adversarial' engagement, in which 'fair' might reasonably imply equal numbers of women and men; and, at the other end, a 'conciliatory' meeting, wherein the meaning of fairness would be much more about being able and willing to compromise. The need for an enrichened discourse in this area is, perhaps, most revealingly confirmed by the current practice wisdom that advises the sole mediator, who feels sympathy towards one party and antipathy to the other, to consider the involvement of a co-worker (see 'resisting alliances', Parkinson, 1997, p.376).

Finally, in describing how they had been unfairly treated, some men referred to allegations of violence that they saw as unfounded.

> It seemed just because she had lied her way into a Women's Refuge and lied about beatings (with no evidence to back up allegations of mental, physical and sexual abuse) she seemed to automatically have the mediator's and the court's sympathy,

although it is important to add that many more women than men made reference to violence or intimidation. Mediators and related professionals need to be aware that some allegations of abuse may be untrue or exaggerated, although they will also want to hold in mind both the wider picture of unreported violence and intimidation, and the propensity of perpetrators to deny their crimes. Haynes (1993, pp.35–7) provides a poignant example of how, as a practising mediator, he had missed the signs of abuse and failed to provide opportunities for the woman to disclose that she was being repeatedly intimidated by her partner. In such circumstances, the pursuance of fairness makes a particularly hollow sound.

## Keeping to Agreements

The question of how men and women might be expected to differ in terms of their respective capacity and willingness to keep to mediation agreements is both epistemologically taxing and politically fraught. Nevertheless, in the context of fairness, it is an important question and one that should not be avoided, although a detailed exposition is beyond the parameters of this essay. One key line of argument would be that the two sexes are significantly different in their responses because of a wider, socialised predilection towards rule-breaking on the part of men. Empirical evidence for such a position would include the much greater propensity for males to infract the criminal-legal code: 34 per cent of men born in 1953, compared with only 8 per cent of women, had been convicted of a standard list offence before the age of 40 (Home Office, 2000, paras. 9.31 and 9.34 respectively); and 7 per cent of males born in 1953 had served a custodial sentence before the age of 40, compared with less than one per cent of women (Home Office, 2000, paras. 9.35 and 9.36 respectively). In other words, men are four times as likely to come to the attention of the criminal courts and seven times as likely to experience custody, which overall is reserved for more serious offences, than are women. There are many caveats to this argument – 'self-report' studies, for example, have suggested that the gap between women's and men's offending is much narrower than the official figures indicate (Cavadino and Dignan, 1997, p.279) – but it would not be unreasonable to conclude that the impact of differential conformity deserves further exploration in the mediation literature.

A further theoretical resource for exploring the differences between men and women in this context might be offered by works concerned with an 'ethic of care' (Gilligan, 1982; Larrabee, 1993). The idea that there might be, at least, two 'voices' to consider in moral reasoning – one a patriarchal predilection for justice, impartiality, universal principle and individual rights, the other giving an emphasis to appropriate, situated responses, relationship and care – has been the subject of extensive debate within a wide range of fields of study. Applying this notion to the question of whether or not women and men might differ in their respective desire to keep to mediation agreements is obviously complicated but it might be reasonable to say that men would be more likely to insist on the 'letter', whereas women might be predisposed to be more flexible, open to compromise, with a sharper eye on the 'spirit' of the agreement. Paradoxically, this difference could be interpreted as a greater propensity on the part of fathers to stick to the arrangements made at mediation, in the sense of the significance they might give to the detail of the agreement reached. However, given the realities of childcare, especially when children begin to focus their interests outside the home and its relationships, a preference for negotiation and flexibility might be much more apposite. Men might thus be expected to be less resilient in the face of, inevitable, diversions from the original contract and, as a consequence, more likely to break the spirit of the agreement – which is to maintain contact, in the child's interests – in the longer term. Obviously this is a question deserving of much more exacting study and detailed analysis. Nevertheless, it is reasonable to conclude that the possibility of different approaches to thinking about what is right, good and fair looks to be a useful addition to the conceptual resources available.

To some readers the issue of 'keeping to agreements' may appear rather an odd one to raise, after all both parties would rightly be expected to have the child's interests at the forefront of their concerns so why should mediation agreements be regarded as such fragile entities? The answer, of course, is that many parents do not appear to put their children first, for a variety of reasons including, perhaps most importantly on the part of men, a desire to 'battle on' regardless. Such individual struggles are framed by wider, structural factors and, within a society that remains oppressive to women, the playing field is far from level. The motivation of men to avoid maintenance payments, coupled with the loopholes in the *Child Support Act 1991* that allow them to do so, place women in an unenviable position. As already mentioned in chapter 2, maintenance is only payable out of the father's earned income, with capital and other assets as a rule being ignored by the Child Support Agency, so that it is quite possible for relatively wealthy individuals to avoid their financial responsibilities, given some rudimentary level of business know-how (it is acknowledged that parents may also apply to the court for 'lump sum' payments for specified needs, although, again, there are many ways in which financial circumstances may be manipulated and portrayed to the father's advantage).

## The Cost of Contact

> It's a pity that people like myself and my daughter are not given any 'protection' from the likes of my ex-husband. He has never been held accountable for what he did and it seems 'allowed' to desecrate a child's family life. The consequences that have followed for myself and my daughter have been devastating and I feel we've had no protection from the legal services whatsoever.

As discussed earlier in this chapter, the father's 'right to contact' is regularly afforded priority even in cases involving serious concerns about safety. Contact may be 'supervised' and/or take place on neutral territory – 'contact centres are often employed for this purpose', see Simpson (1994) – as ways of guarding against abuse but, more often than not, the wishes and interests of mothers are still subjugated to the principle of paternal contact being inherently beneficial and, indeed, rightful. Furthermore, the father's exercise of his right to contact is not always matched by fulfilment of his responsibility under the law to support his children financially and figures from the Centre for Research in Social Policy at Loughborough University, suggesting that the cost of bringing up a child from birth to age seventeen is about £54,000, bring home the potential impact of not contributing towards their maintenance (Murray, 2000). In the Essex study there were many poignant illustrations of just how frustrating, unfair and stressful such inequities can appear:

> I feel that it's caused me more hassle and upset than its worth. Mediation meant I had to sit with someone who abused me and then expected me to talk sensibly with him. It forced me to let my kids go to him so that my eldest son is becoming a replica of him. ...Why can't I just have my kids without them seeing their father? He doesn't pay anything to me for their upkeep and I'm expected to let them go. This stinks.

In a number of cases, 'agreements' had been reached despite expressed concerns by the mother about the likely effects of contact and, indeed, when there may have been evidence to suggest that the children did not want to see their father:

> Nobody would listen...I asked for another hearing to see how the boys had coped, bearing in mind he had made no contact for six months and any phone calls were abusive and shouting at the boys. Neither child wants to see their father. They lean out of the window and tell him to go away. Thankfully, there is no more access and it has been left up to the boys if and when they wish to make contact,

and this key issue of how mediators do and might ascertain the child's viewpoint will be considered further in chapter 6.

In appraising the cost of contact it is helpful to address the effects that a woman's primary responsibility for child care can have. There are a number of key contexts to consider here but, for the purposes of this book, it is sufficient to examine the difficulties of establishing and maintaining a new intimate relationship. There are a number of strands to this: first, the chances of meeting a new partner may be restricted by child care necessities and limited employment opportunities; second, a new partner may be wary of the ex-husband; and, third, making a new relationship, in practice, is likely to involve the concurrent establishment of links between the new partner and one or more children – in cases where the relationship becomes serious enough for cohabitation, such complexities, of course, become unavoidable. Against this background, the additional difficulties that may be associated with the maintenance of contact might be formidable, although this is not to suggest that there might be no benefits of contact – staying contact, for example, could allow the new couple time and space to form and develop their relationship, without the demands of child care. In contrast, the non-resident father faces problems of a very different order of severity. Again, these are matters that mediators need to be sensitive to in their quest for 'fairness' and the following words are presented as a powerful illustration of just how difficult it can be for women to maintain new relationships alongside ongoing contact between their children and ex-partner:

> My ex-husband expects to be allowed to enter the house whenever he feels like it. He expects me to do this because he says he has a right to see his children in their own home...I have met someone else and he is already spending more and more time here with me and the kids, so we want to move and buy a place together. Our nightmare is that my ex- will still insist on coming to the house. I know we can get a solicitor and have him stopped but he will just use this as an excuse to stir up trouble with the kids, who have got used to him visiting. I don't know what to do for the best.

Estimating the 'cost of contact' may also be approached by identifying the additional work that mothers are often obliged to undertake in order to ensure that contact takes place. This may involve helping with the transport – taking children to railway or bus stations, or via, sometimes, lengthy car journeys – paying towards fares, telephone bills and the like. However, there may be other, much less obvious 'expenses' that bear heavily on women who are also struggling to combine a childcare role with full- or part-time employment. Backett (1987), for example, describes how mothers in intact families not only provide most of the care but also help the father to relate to his children by interpreting their needs and emotions. Kraemer (1995) has, similarly, argued that men learn how to parent through the cues provided by their partner which means that, while mothers may have a direct relationship with their children, fatherhood is dependent, to a large extent, on the active co-operation of mothers. If this is true, then there are important implications for relationships following parental separation. Fathers who for years may have taken for granted the willingness of their ex-partners to maintain a 'bridge' to their children will suddenly experience a sharp disjuncture. Smart (1999, pp.103–104), drawing on Backett's research, points out that a mother may simply no longer be prepared or able to continue in this role and that the father may, as a result, be required to learn new ways of relating to his children and, indeed, to his children's mother – as opposed to 'his wife'. Many fathers may resent or misunderstand this need for change on their part: many may become angry, depressed or seek escape by ceasing contact with their children. Either way, the cost to mothers may be considerable.

The vast majority of writers in the field of fatherhood would acknowledge that some fathers are best forgotten, although most would also assume that 'some' would represent only a very small number. There is an interesting parallel here with the near consensus around the use of imprisonment in that most experts in penality and criminal justice would accept that there is a limited, residual need for the custodial containment and/or punishment of 'serious', 'dangerous' or persistent offenders, even though the meaning of 'limited' is left unclear (Blackstone, 1990, p.54):

> By their actions some men and a few women in all societies forfeit their right to their liberty. Prisons will always be needed for the small number of human beings who cannot control their aggression and who behave violently towards others, or whose uncontrollable greed undermines the society in which they operate.

However, the number of potential candidates for custody, the overwhelming majority of whom are male, appears to be rather large – in 1998, a total of 37,100 offenders were sentenced to indictable offences of violence against the person, a further 4,600 for sexual offences, 5,600 for robbery and 31,100 for burglary (Home Office, 2000, Table 7.2) – an understanding that suggests the need for a review of the maxim that 'prison is only for the very few'. The point to be made here is that both serious criminal activity and abusive fathering are frequently pushed to the margins of lay and expert awareness and opinion: both are presented as matters of low incidence and, consequently, of lesser significance. There is evidence to support an alternative stance, a perspective that regards male transgression in both arenas as a much more common phenomenon: such evidence would include the propensity of males to offend and experience incarceration, and the high incidence of 'domestic violence' and its long-standing and pervasive representation as being less, rather than more, serious than other forms of assault.

The 'costs of contact' for mothers may be considerable but it is also important to take into account the adverse effects of contact for children with the non-resident parent, alongside the more positive outcomes.

Although a detailed exposition of this question is beyond the parameters of this book it is important to emphasise the difficulties involved in deciding when contact is likely to be of benefit and when it is not, and to cite Quinton's (1996) conclusion that the 'quality' of relationship is a more significant factor than whether or not contact takes place *per se*.

Finally, a handful of fathers and mothers in the Essex study described unfair treatment because of their psychiatric condition:

> I feel the proceedings were loaded against me, having a psychiatric record. This was the direct impression presented by the Court Welfare Officer...Yes, as a psychiatric patient, I want absolutely nothing to do with my son's mother who caused my initial breakdown,

which raises the general question of how mediators approach the assessment of risk in cases where mental health and related issues are present. The cost of contact in such cases may require an especially exacting appraisal and, as the following words from a mother convey, it is possible that safety is not always given sufficient attention:

> I am supposed to take them to the centre just so he can terrify them (and me). This is just asking for trouble. Why does he have the right to do this just because he is the children's father?

There is some evidence to suggest that psychiatric illness, ironically, may also be, at least in part, a result of not being able to have enough contact: Kitson and Holmes (1992) suggest that non-resident fathers may be vulnerable to such problems if their wishes for contact with their children after divorce are not met.

## Resident Fathers

The fact that, after divorce or parental separation, children are usually cared for by their mother is well-established. However, it is important to recognise that this is not always the case and that sometimes children may be looked after by their father or by other adults. In the Essex study, for example, 16 per cent of fathers had this responsibility, compared with 80 per cent of mothers – in 3 per cent of families the children were cared for by foster parents or family members and in the small number of remaining cases the study children were separated. Hetherington and Stanley-Hogan (1997, p.205) report that some 14 per cent of divorcing fathers are awarded sole custody in the United States, while DeMaris and Grief (1997, p.146) predict that the phenomenon of fathers as sole parents is likely to become a great deal more common in future.

The case of resident fathers has attracted little previous attention (Adams, 1996) and there is clearly a need for extensive qualitative and quantitative research. There is a literature concerned with fathers who are primary caregivers – their partners acting as 'providers' – and there may be pointers here for the construction of studies of sole male parents. The similarities and differences between the execution of carework by women and by men in such circumstances looks to be an especially attractive area of study and it is possible to say that there is some, albeit limited, empirical evidence to support theses of both difference and similitude. Ehrensaft (1995), for example, reports that fathers in her study of American parents were equally capable in child care but were also able to maintain a sense of separation between themselves and their children. Mothers, in contrast, had a much greater feeling of emotional proximity with their children – a sense of sameness or common interest – even when they were pursuing high-powered and demanding careers in public life. Other research has emphasised the similarities between male and female primary carers: Lupton and Barclay (1997), in their interview study conducted in Australia, found that men were able to develop a 'maternal thinking' that allowed them to form an intense, affective relationship with their children and the authors cite research by Grbich (1995) who suggests that, when men do adopt a front-line, nurturing role, they do so in ways that are very similar to the traditional maternal pattern (Lupton and Barclay, 1997, p.134). Small-scale research by Dowling and Gorell-Barnes (2000, p.19) suggests that men are able to parent effectively and the authors warn of the danger in generalising about what lone fathers are able to provide.

One intriguing question for further research might therefore be to explore the usefulness of traditional concepts of 'mothering' in the arena of sole male parenting. Also, the part to be played by the non-resident mother – in effect, the rationale or justification for her 'right to contact' – might be considered.

For mediators, the challenge of resident fathers would appear to be whether or not to apply the same set of 'standard' packages of contact as they do when mothers have the primary caring role. If it is believed that children need their mother more than their father, or that mothering is something that only mothers can do or do satisfactorily, then it would follow that mediators and other court professionals might be likely to afford greater weight to the importance of contact between children and non-resident mothers. One example from the Essex study provides the following, illuminating account:

> I think as a dad looking after his kids people have to take a second look because it's usually the mother who does it but once they hear you talking about what you do to make sure they are looked after properly it's alright...The mediator was fine though, she was relaxed and open about it and didn't write me off just because I'm male...she listened and I think it must have also helped that my solicitor was a woman because she accepted that I could make a home for my children as well. Maybe it would not have been so easy if my ex- had been totally well, she has depression and is on medication for it,

that raises the question of how factors such as psychiatric and physical illness might bear upon decision-making in this context.

Under section 8 of the *Children Act 1989*, a residence order may be made in favour of more than one person, if this is seen to be in the child's interests, and, occasionally, courts do make 'split' residence orders in favour of both the mother and the father. Sometimes the two parents live separately and sometimes they continue to live in the same household, at least for a period of time: both types of arrangement are encompassed by the notion of 'joint residence'. The case of joint residence, whether the two parties are sharing accommodation or not, involves fathers in a much more central mode of parenting and such arrangements have been shown to offer benefits to both parents (Bender, 1994), although children may experience significant difficulties if they are obliged to witness disputes between their parents. Arguably this is much more likely in cases where the household is shared and, in such circumstances, residence with one parent may be the preferred option: one Essex study father describes it thus:

> At first we tried living in the same house hoping it would be best for the kids. We tried to keep our distance but in the end we just couldn't stop arguing about money and getting on each others nerves so I moved out into rented accommodation nearby...I don't think the kids ever accepted the break-up until I did leave and neither of us wanted to get back together so in the long term view it's got to be for the best.

The field of joint residence where both parents continue to share family accommodation is dramatically under-researched and looks to be a priority for exploratory study. The availability of baseline quantitative data would make a vital addition to our knowledge and discourse in this area:

Hill, for example, is able to assert that the 'vast majority' of fathers live in the family household after a relationship ends (Hill, 2000a) while the Essex study reveals that only a tiny minority of parents continued to share accommodation. At least in part, such striking contrasts can be accounted for by, *inter alia*, changes over time, but it would be most helpful to have some firmer empirical ground on which to base our discussions and policies. Perhaps one of the key conceptual outcomes of such study would be a re-appraisal and consequent elaboration of the meanings we attach to notions of 'the end of relationship' and 'separation'.

Finally, there is value in placing the widespread prioritisation of mothering in an historical context – this provides a useful counter to the view that nothing can change – and, as Haynes (1993, p.74) points out, up to the turn of the twentieth century children normally stayed with their father when couples divorced:

> That was probably because, in earlier times, children were seen as chattels or economic units. With the introduction of universal education they ceased to be economic units and became economic liabilities. Along with this change the courts introduced the concept of 'welfare of the child' and began almost automatically to award the custody of the children to the mother.

Given this longer term perspective it is, perhaps, easier to predict that the present situation, wherein between 11 and 14 per cent of children live with their fathers after divorce, is likely to change over the coming decades (Dowling and Gorell-Barnes, 2000, p.16). The pressure for mediators to review and adapt their practices is thus likely to build in the future.

### Conclusion

The absence of a clear picture of what purposeful, post-divorce fatherhood might look like is unhelpful to mediators, fathers and mothers, and, in this regard, the pioneering work concerned with 'generative' fathering (Snarey, 1993; Hawkins and Dollahite, 1997) is to be warmly welcomed. Without such a picture mediators may fall back on a standardised settlement based on accommodating the father's right to have contact, regardless of the particularities of the individual case. Non-resident fathers who want to be much more closely involved in raising their children will doubtless be angry and frustrated by their consequent marginalisaton in mediation's traditional presumptions and processes. Their sense of unfairness will arise from an apparent inertia in the family court system, reflecting wider beliefs about the relative importance of maternal and paternal roles. In child-centred mediation, wherein the question of financial provision is rarely discussed, fathers may feel especially marginalised, given their traditional 'provider' role – even unemployed fathers who provide the childcare regard themselves as 'failed providers' rather than successful childcarers (Hill, 2000a).

On the other hand, the misuses and abuses of power perpetrated by many fathers should not be lost sight of. There is much to commend the argument that men have been allowed to slip their responsibilities, within the ascendant culture of individualism and sexism. The cost to women of maintaining contact between children and their fathers is often heavy and deserves to be recognised, alongside the already considerable difficulties that lone mothers encounter. The Essex study findings include many examples of apparent insensitivity on the part of fathers to the needs and wishes of their ex-partners. The extra burden of care carried by women and the related limits imposed on their opportunities to build an independent future, with or without a new partner, often appear to be taken for granted, or otherwise dismissed, by men. Mothers are all too frequently presented as culpable, for the marital dissolution and for any difficulties that subsequently arise. The vitriolic and largely uncompromising public reaction to the Child Support Agency, notwithstanding its evident shortcomings, surely has been and continues to be indicative of an unwillingness on the part of men to put the interests of children and their main carers above their own. With clear parallels to the use of 'domestic' violence, that reaction has included serious threats to and the direct intimidation of CSA personnel – Murray reports the abuse suffered by Faith Boardman, the present head of the agency, who feared that two fathers might push her under a train, while waiting at a railway station, and also describes the throwing of bricks through office windows at the previous headquarters in Dudley and the additional protective arrangements made at the new site in Newcastle (Murray, 2000). Such actions need to be held in mind alongside both the vociferous lobbying executed by groups currently promoting the images of 'new man' and 'new father', and the apparent receptivity of government. Male ascendancy is a project evidently far from exhausted and if Erikson's idea of 'generativity' – contributing to the well-being and development of the new generation – is to have any worthwhile application, then fathers will need to work towards the creation and sustenance of a social environment that is much less oppressive to women. Dominance, insensitivity, self-absorption and violence are best left to the past and the idea of fathers having some unassailable 'right to contact' might similarly be resigned to history.

Although co-mediation will be explored further in chapter 6, it is appropriate to suggest here that the employment of two workers might usefully be reviewed, with especial attendances to, first, the potential impact upon the balance of power and, second, the ramifications for anti-sexist strategies and practice.

There are lessons here also for user/consumer studies within the mediation and related fields. Asking fathers whether they have been treated fairly may generate responses that spring from three very different understandings of the question: first, a conceptualisation inextricably connected with the informant's sensitivity to the claims and politics of 'new fatherhood', within the context of normative expectations held and promoted by mediators and other professionals; second, a more limited construction concerned with the mediator's professional style; and, finally, a view of fairness associated with differences of, *inter alia*, race, ethnicity, sexual orientation, gender and class.

# 4    Mediation and Violence

> I felt uncomfortable anyway having to sit in the same room as the man that assaulted me and who I'd had arrested for ABH, harassment and violence while entering my house.

The above words capture the fear that many women experience during mediation. The apprehension is real and demands to be acknowledged, rather than qualified or smoothed away. With this in mind, the title of this chapter was carefully chosen: the adjective 'domestic' has been very deliberately avoided, on the grounds that its inclusion might detract from the seriousness of the criminal offences involved and, indeed, from the pain and trepidation experienced by women survivors. The trauma from prior experience of battering and the consequent fear of further assault are much too significant in the accounts given by many women who attended mediation to risk any such softening, soothing or blurring. It is acknowledged that 'domestic violence' has gained a much higher prominence in recent times, as a substantive area of study and of public policy. The point remains, however, that the descriptor 'domestic' appears to offer room for distraction, obfuscation and mitigation, taken within the historical and contemporary contexts of women's oppression by men. The decision to avoid using the term has been taken after exhaustive study and in full recognition of the efforts to find alternative terminology made by other writers in this field, some of whom have chosen to employ the words 'domestic violence' (Johnson, 1995; Walklate, 2000). 'Domestic' may also be interpreted more widely, so as to denote both child and elder abuse (Phillipson and Biggs, 1995; Adelman et al., 1999), other manifestations of family violence. Because of the close association between the constructs 'domestic' and 'family', and the institutionalised homophobia that maintains family as heterosexual property, the term 'domestic' may also serve to marginalise violence that occurs between homosexual partners (Renzetti, 1992; Davies and Neal, 1996). In attempting to avoid such pitfalls, scholars in this field have adopted a number of alternative terms: 'spouse abuse' (Kandel-Englander, 1997), 'partner violence' (O'Leary and Murphy, 1999), 'partner abuse' (Hudson, 1990) and, more recently, 'intimate partner violence' (Bachman, 1999) have all appeared in the literature. Finally, the apparent unwillingness in the UK to employ an appropriate descriptor for violence that does not involve family members ('non-domestic') may, arguably, contribute towards the implicit construction of 'domestic' violence as less serious – in effect, as an inferior relation of 'real' violence. The expansion of current terminology would be relatively straightforward – 'street', 'domestic' and 'pan' (denoting perpetrators who commit violent acts against *both* family and non-family members) categories of violence are customarily employed in the United States (Kandel-Englander, 1997, pp.16–32) – although there are difficulties stemming from the fact that both 'street' and 'domestic' carry connotations of location *and* relationship. Perhaps it would be preferable to aim for a typology based on the relationship between offender and survivor, rather than where the offence took place. In this case, 'street' would encompass violence perpetrated by strangers, acquaintances and peers while 'domestic' would refer to intimate partner violence (IPV), and elder or child abuse. 'Pan' would include offenders who were violent towards their partners and to strangers. One advantage of this categorisation – in general terms and for the specific purposes of this chapter – would be the recognition that 'IPV' occurs inside and outside the home, that is in both private and public space.

The relationships between domestic violence and child abuse have received limited attention in the literature, although this is changing fairly rapidly: a primary conceptual distinction to be made is between the effects on children of witnessing and living with abuse against their mother or surrogate female carer (this may appropriately be construed as child abuse), and the association of child and partner abuse in terms of the probability that male perpetrators will commit both types of offence. Key sources would include: Child Abuse Studies Unit (1993); Mullender and Morley (1994); Attala *et al.* (1995); Stanley (1997); Knapp (1998); and Cattanach (2000).

In the context of contact arrangements between children and the absent parent, there is evidence of a growing recognition of the association of child and partner abuse. Hester and Radford (1996, p.19), for example, point out that:

> ...child contact gives fathers the opportunity to continue to abuse, harass and to exert control over women and children. Violent men may be poor parents. Failure to consider the impact of domestic violence upon children puts children at risk of abuse, neglect and poor standards of care.

Findings from the British Crime Survey (Mirrlees-Black, 1999) suggest that some 23 per cent of women are survivors of domestic assault over their lifetime, although it is widely recognised that this figure is likely to be an underestimate (Home Office, 2000). The comparable figure for men is 15 per cent which, at first glance, might suggest a near parity of experience. However, a more detailed scrutiny of the BCS findings indicates that women are much more seriously affected than their male counterparts, facing twice the risk of injury and being more likely to experience repeated assaults. Other indications of difference include the finding from the 'Criminal Statistics for England and Wales, 1997' that 47 per cent of women homicide victims were killed by their partners, compared to 8 per cent of men (Home Office, 1998). Kilpatrick (1993) suggests that, in the United States, some 40 per cent of all rapes are committed by husbands or other male partners. Kandel-Englander (1997, p.24) draws attention to differences in terms of both culpability and intent:

> Whereas a man hitting a woman is likely to cause injury, a woman hitting a man is less likely to do so. Both men and women are typically aware of this different potential for injury, and this awareness is a factor in the determination of abuse. That is, violence is more abusive if the perpetrators know that they will probably injure their victims...Perhaps the most significant difference between male and female spousal violence is, however, intent. Women and men may behave violently toward their mates for very different reasons. Most notably, men are more likely to hit offensively; women self-defensively.

Overall, it is reasonable to conclude that violence affects the lives of many women in society and that it is a particularly common and traumatic issue for women.

Aggregated data may conceal significant differences and it is important to recognise the higher risks faced by women living in poor households and by younger women. The British Crime Survey found that 10 per cent of women aged 16 to 19 and 9 per cent of women aged 20 to 24 had been assaulted during the previous year, compared to an average of 4 per cent for women of all ages. No significant differences were reported in regard to ethnic origin, although other studies have found that black and Asian women may experience additional pressures (Mama, 1989; Adams, 1998). However, a key finding of the British Crime Survey is that women who are separating from their partner are at much higher risk: 22 per cent of separated women were assaulted in the previous year by their partners or ex-partners. This is of central importance to all those concerned with family court policy and practice: it suggests that at least one fifth of women attending mediation and similar joint meetings with their ex-partners may have been assaulted within the prior twelve months. There is a strong association between separation and violence and, overall, women are, perhaps, five times (a precise comparison would need to control for 'age') as likely to have been assaulted than their male counterparts. It is also apparent that women and men separate for different reasons: Dowling and Gorell Barnes (2000) found that, in their research sample, the most frequent single reason for separating given by women was 'violence' while the corresponding reason offered by men was that they had 'fallen in love' with another woman (p.44). In the mediation context, there is evidence from the United States to suggest that violence may be much more commonplace than has hitherto been believed: Parkinson (1997, p.51) describes a mediation project which was prohibited from accepting 'victims' of violence – this resulted in some 60 per cent of potential service users being excluded from the project, although it is important to add that a number of women so excluded had, according to project personnel, expressed a wish to take part in mediation in spite of the history of abuse.

Violence is perpetrated against women within a number of phaseal contexts linked to separation. First, men may abuse their partners for many years before the woman decides, and finds the strength and support, to leave the relationship. In other words, violence may have a causal connection with separation. Second, the initial announcement of the desire to leave may 'precipitate' further, or, in relationships that had not previously been violent, primary, attacks. Once again, there is a pressing need for vigilance in the use of terminology: 'precipitate' (or 'trigger') might lead one to believe that the woman's decision to leave had somehow 'caused' the violence – whereas the cause is with the offender. Mahoney (1991) urges the use of the words 'separation assault' to describe the violence employed by men as a strategy for denying women their independence, while Ptacek (1999, p.79) cites a wealth of research evidence supporting the contention that men are violent as a means of resisting women's struggle for autonomy. Violence is thus not only a feature of male power and control but also a characteristic of male responses to women's attempts to resist and break free. Third, violence and intimidation may continue for many years after the separation: there may be early attempts to force the woman to return to the relationship, followed by a long-standing pattern of threat and occasional assault. This tripartite conceptualisation of 'separation violence' is not shared by all other writers in the field: Johnston and Campbell (1993), for example, define it as uncharacteristic of previous interactional patterns, in other words they see value in distinguishing cases where no prior violence has taken place and limit the currency of the term to violence precipitated by the declaration by one party of their intention to finish the relationship. The authors suggest that such cases may benefit from mediation, even though violence has transpired.

## Violence: Process and Event

Much of the discourse in this area tends to represent violence as an event, an abrupt punctuation of an otherwise peaceful prose, and it is important to highlight the pitfalls that such representation produces. Perhaps the most obvious is the danger of conceptualising 'survival' as something that only needs to be done on discrete occasions, rather than as a long-term strategy and process for and of self-protection. Women enter intimate relationships with men within a wider context of power differences and oppressions. Until quite recently the notion of 'rape' within marriage was simply unheard of: the sexual dominion of men over women in this context was unquestioned and the issue of consent afforded no legal relevance whatsoever. Themes of male dominance and aggression against their wives, lovers and partners have significant vocal and literary histories and all individual women commencing relations with men will, to some extent, be aware of the risk. So, in this sense, violence is a part of every such relationship and women are obliged to find ways of coping with it: for example, through the adoption of beliefs such as 'all men are not the same' or 'he isn't the violent type'. The initial distractions of romance and enhanced sexual activity may also resign the issue of violence to lower points on the woman's agenda. As the relationship proceeds, such convictions and diversions may become less important, particularly if intimations or threats of abuse begin to occur. Once assault becomes likely or happens, the woman's assumptive world (Young, 1977) changes – understandings drawn from women's wider experience come to hold a particular 'truth' for the individual woman concerned and illusions, if not shattered, become much harder to preserve. The prospect of further violent incidents has to be recognised and strategies of avoidance speedily put in place. There is evidence to suggest, however, that such strategies prove ineffective in many cases and that many women suffer repeated incidents of violence – Stelman (1993), for example, refers to police research showing that, '...on average, a woman endures 30 to 35 assaults before she contacts the police' (p.193): similarly, data from the British Crime Survey suggests that previous domestic assault is the best predictor of further attacks with 35 per cent of households suffering a second incident within five weeks of the first (Home Office, 2000). Women who do decide to bring their plight to the attention of public agencies often do so after a long history of abuse and it is crucial that their testimonies are heard and taken seriously. Although it is reasonable to argue that progress has been achieved in this regard, particularly in terms of police responses, there is evidence that further improvement is urgently needed. The following words from a participant in the Essex study demonstrate the frustration felt by women who, having summoned the courage to do something, find that their fears are apparently denied.

> The first mediator didn't take the violent marriage into account. So after going to the police and going to court she made me feel I was wasting everyone's time...

It would be wrong to suggest that the foregoing series of phases is something which all women who survive violence are somehow obliged to pass through or that all women's awareness and experience are the same. Sometimes, for example, women know that their partner-to-be has a history of aggression and yet proceed with building the relationship, as the following account ('Jane' in Cameron, 1991, p.38) illustrates:

> When myself and my husband formed our relationship, I was quite aware of his past behaviour. I was actually aware that if we did decide to form a relationship together, violence could occur. That was something I chose to ignore, as I believed in my mind that he would never hurt me through violence. I later came to learn that I was no exception to the violence that my husband held within himself, and I started to experience the aggressive side to his personality.

In this case the woman initially feels that she is 'different' or 'special' – a feeling that could be an idealising concomitant of 'being in love' – and that this personal status might be sufficient to prevent violence. Previous survivors of her partner's attacks are thus constructed as 'less worthy' of her man's affections and, arguably, 'more deserving' of his violence. Her illusions were rudely shattered. The general point to be made, however, is that women's experiences and perceptions of violence from their partner or ex-partner may depend on a wide range of factors. On the other hand, there does appear to be a number of recurrent themes in the testimonies of women survivors and it would be important for mediators to have received appropriate education and training in this field: this would include close attention to: the views of women survivors of violence – see, for example, Mullender and Hague (2000); strategies of dominance, abuse and justification employed by perpetrators – Morran (1995), Russell and Frohberg (1995), Burton *et al.* (1998), Jukes (1999); and effective approaches to risk assessment/ management – Walby and Myhill (2000).

Because an 'assault' is traditionally seen as a single incident, one of the dangers of employing the notion of 'separation assault' is the (possible) implication that separation is an event, rather than a process. This would be a significant mistake although, as pointed out by Rodgers and Pryor (1998, p.51) in their impressive review of contemporary research, not an uncommon one. Similarly, it would be misleading to conceptualise violence in this context as an event or unrelated series of events. In other words, violence needs to be perceived as a process – albeit one punctuated by episodes of more intense or overt abuse. 'Separation abuse' or 'separation violence' might therefore be more exacting and useful ideas within an assembly of conceptual resources in this field. Both separation and violence are processes, often lasting many years before the divorce, during the break(s) in cohabitation and continuing on into the parental interactions concerned with financial matters as well as contact and residence arrangements for children.

**The Safety and Efficacy of Mediation**

Women who have suffered violence are likely to experience great anxiety about meeting their ex-partner. They may fear further violence and/or be distressed at the prospect of having to share a common space with their assailant, because of the memories of victimisation, anger and feelings of revulsion, made all the more acute by their 'relationship' context. To be physically, sexually and mentally abused is bad enough: to suffer at the hands of a loved one is arguably a great deal worse. Such violence is all the more destructive: it marks the perversion of (perceptions of) prior protectiveness and care. To have to 'meet' with one's abuser therefore demands considerable bravery and resilience but, in inviting women to mediation, this is what is being asked for, albeit unwittingly. Although the purpose of the meeting may be otherwise defined, the issue of violence is firmly on the agenda for many women and, no doubt, this is why some refuse the offer. However, it would be far too simple to suggest that this apparent freedom to refuse somehow completes the debate: after all, women may feel obliged to at least show willing in moves to arrange contact between father and children. Furthermore, many, if not most, will genuinely want to have some form of agreement in place despite the difficulties and fears presented by the prospect of mediation.

The difficulties and risks of attempting mediation in cases where violence is a factor are well-documented: Liebmann (1998, p.50) states that mediation is inappropriate if there are threats or fear of violence, while Mullender and Hague (2000), in a major review of what women survivors of domestic violence think about the quality and shortcomings of the public services they receive, report the fears expressed by women's organisations that survivors may be pressurised into mediation and other joint meetings with their abusers. 'Looking to the Future: Mediation and the Ground for Divorce', the government's White Paper (Lord Chancellor's Department, 1995), also expressed the view that mediation was inappropriate in cases involving domestic violence and, as already mentioned in this chapter, there has been a great deal of related debate and legislation in the United States. The question, therefore, of why mediation appears to be happening in many cases where violence is on the agenda attains a new prominence: put sharply, if the accepted, professional wisdom is not to offer mediation in such circumstances, why does it occur? In part the reply must be that cases are not properly screened for violence or not screened at all, but this begs the next query of why the issue appears not to be taken sufficiently seriously. The plot becomes even more difficult to follow when the availability of alternatives such as 'shuttle mediation' (Parkinson, 1997, p.80) is considered: mediation does not have to involve a face-to-face meeting, it can be facilitated by the mediator moving between rooms in which each party is respectively ensconced. This form of mediation is recognised as a more appropriate mode when aggression or fear are present and, although the risks of violence before and after the mediation meeting would still need to be addressed, the use of shuttle mediation should enhance safety. It is fair to say, therefore, that the lack of a viable option is unlikely to be a sustainable reply to the question of why conjoint, and especially, face-to-face mediation is so prevalent in cases where domestic violence is present.

The protection of women in cases where violence is involved is clearly the most compelling reason for not proceeding with mediation. However, it is also important to consider the weight of two other arguments against its employment in such cases: first, that the parties are less likely to reach agreement during mediation; and, second, that any agreement achieved is less likely to stand the test of time. Robinson (1999, p.133) cites earlier work by Irving and Benjamin (1995) who suggest that the probability of 'outcome failure' may be greater in cases where 'current and ongoing family violence' is present, although it is unclear how the measure is being defined – as 'agreement', 'duration' or as a conflation of the two? There is good reason to demand greater precision. Paradoxically, parents may be more, rather than less likely to reach 'agreement' in mediation, although such agreements are perhaps unlikely to be robust. There is evidence, for example, from the Essex study that some women who had suffered abuse participated in an apparent settlement, in which really they had little faith, largely to escape the intimidatory tactics of their ex-partner. The following words eloquently make the point:

> There was no way he was going to keep the arrangements anyway because he has always done what he wants and had his own way...and since the kids have also stopped going. I was shaking inside but everyone seemed to want a happy ending so I went along with it but just to get it over with as quickly as possible.

This testimony offers an illuminating insight into the complexity of mediation, with a number of factors serving to shape the meaning and significance of 'agreement', one of which is the woman's response to feeling unsafe. It is reasonable to suggest, therefore, that considerable caution would need to be exercised in attempts to gauge the efficacy of mediation solely in terms of 'agreements reached' – some, if not many will be 'paper' rather than 'real'. Furthermore, tracing the relationship between 'agreement', as an outcome measure, and the incidence of partner violence is likely to present many pitfalls for the unwary. It is also fair to say that the distinction between achieving agreement and its duration, as outcome measures, is not always sufficiently clear in the literature, perhaps reflecting a tendency to assume that both measures are similarly associated with the presence or absence of violence. There may indeed be a close correlation but, at this point of writing, it is only possible to say that the matter needs to be the subject of further enquiry.

Finally, it may be helpful to recall the definition of 'separation violence' employed by Johnston and Campbell (1993), discussed earlier in this chapter, as 'uncharacteristic of previous behaviour' – in other words, the violence commences when one party says they want to leave the relationship – and the authors' consequent proposal that such cases may benefit from mediation. There appear to be dangers in this way of defining separation violence: first, an 'incidental' rather than a processual model of violence may be promulgated; second, there may be a tendency to blame the party making the declaration to end the relationship; and, third, the tenet that violence and mediation should not be allowed to mix may be undermined. This is not to deny the contention that some cases may well fit the definition offered by Johnston and Campbell. The point being made is that such cases are likely to be few and far between, given the research evidence to hand, and that the risks probably outweigh any likely gains.

## The Sharing of Court Waiting Rooms Before Mediation

> I think that this was awful as I have a past of violence with this man and I am at a court to explain the harm he was causing to my children and yet for half an hour I was allowed to be stared at across the room and emotionally battered.

While waiting to be called to the mediation session, parents often find themselves sharing the same waiting area at court (some 80 per cent in the Essex study). This experience is also faced in the context of other court procedures and, as a consequence, the issues addressed in this section of the chapter have a much wider coverage than mediation alone. As so powerfully illustrated by the words prefacing this section of the chapter, many women find the experience of sharing waiting rooms with their ex-partners especially harrowing.

In the Essex study, 63 per cent of women (compared with 39 per cent of men) had found the sharing of the waiting area a cause for concern and, of these women, 20 per cent (13 per cent of women overall) made explicit reference to a history of violence from their ex-partner. The questionnaire used carries no reference to 'violence', a fact that makes the prevalence of testimonies explicitly naming it all the more significant. Of the remainder of women who had been concerned, most referred to feeling anxious, intimidated, dominated or abused without citing a history of 'violence'. It would not be unreasonable to suggest that many of this group had indeed suffered from physical abuse during the early phases of separation, in addition to prior maltreatment.

Some women evidently find the prospect of sharing the waiting area too much to bear and seek safety wherever they can find it, 'I ran into the toilets when I heard my ex-husband's voice and stayed there until proceedings began', and 'Yes because I was beaten up by my husband and he scares me. I went into the hall area to get away', while others request alternative waiting accommodation: 'I was very concerned about this but expressed my concerns and was able to sit in a small room by myself', and 'I have had to have six injunctions against my husband. Therefore I felt very uncomfortable, my solicitor found an alternative room downstairs eventually'.

However, the Essex study indicates that such availability varies markedly from court to court and that there are often competing demands for accommodation. In such circumstances it is perhaps not surprising that women who find the experience unbearable seek safety wherever they can find it: as preface to, or preparation for the mediation meeting, such humiliating experiences are clearly unacceptable.

A significant proportion of men – about one third – also find the shared waiting area a cause for concern. Their concerns, however, stand in sharp contrast to those given by women: in the main the reasons are the tense atmosphere produced and having to stay in the presence of new partners:

> To be forced to witness the one you still love with the new love in their life right in front of you is absolutely intolerable and shows a lack of compassion.

The sharing of waiting areas at court is difficult to justify given the narratives provided by women in the Essex study. The following words are offered as a symbol of the urgent need to change this practice.

> Yes, I was very nervous as I had never taken my ex-husband to court in 12 years of violence. I was very scared being in the same room as him. By the time the meeting started I was shaking and crying.

Emotional reactions such as this are far from uncommon and raise questions not only about safety but also about the subsequent quality of the mediation event itself. Women so distressed are unlikely to give a good account of themselves and their perception of mediation is also unlikely to be enhanced – that is if such a low priority is being given to what women regard as an important matter. Policy in this area appears to be absent or, at best, insufficiently focused – Home Office (1994, para. 1.21) 'National Standards for Family Court Work', for example, offer the following guidance:

> Accommodation should be separate from that used by convicted and accused persons and should enable the parties to wait separately. Separate

access and rooms should be provided for family court welfare work in buildings in shared use.

The need for separate waiting areas is here afforded very little support, a few words set in a paragraph dedicated to another issue, and it is especially important for government to state a clear position on the matter of accommodation given that family court services operate on county court premises and thus have to argue a legitimate case for changes, often in the face of conflicting demands for accommodation. There is a need for urgent attention to be given to the issue of how women survivors of violence may be protected from the distress and fear associated with having to share court waiting areas with their former partners. Parkinson (1997, p.255) identifies a set of safeguards for practice in this area, including the following precepts:

> If one party is afraid of arriving or leaving the building at the same time as the other party, prior arrangements should be agreed with both parties to enable them to arrive and leave separately. Separate waiting-areas should also be available,

while Hester and Radford (1996, p.31) describe a form of 'shuttle mediation' involving the parents being seen on different days. It is possible, therefore, to conclude that current practices, at least in Essex County Courts, neither conform to extant, protective guidelines nor incorporate the safer modes of mediation available.

## Face to Face With the Enemy: The Perils of Joint Meetings

> Court welfare officers must exercise particular care in cases in which violence between the parties has been alleged. A joint interview must not be convened if it can reasonably be foreseen that the safety or well-being of either party might be jeopardised (Home Office, 1994, s.4.13).

This seemingly unequivocal precept is provided by central government for family court officers who are organising meetings with parents for the purposes of preparing a welfare report under section 7 of the *Children Act 1989*. However, a national survey of family court officers reported that, despite the national standard, only about one half of participants had considered the issue of domestic violence for welfare report meetings and only about a quarter carried out any screening for domestic violence at initial appointments/hearings (Hester *et al.*, 1997). Although the researchers state that these figures suggest an improvement in practices since earlier surveys, it is clear that much more needs to be done, even where a firm message of expectation and accountability has been conveyed by government.

For mediation interviews it is puzzling not to find any comparable guidance for practitioners within the extant national standards. It would be difficult to argue that the risks of and from a history of violence would be any the less. Hester *et al.* report that half of the officers who participated in their study had felt that a systematic screening policy would be of benefit, although many others were concerned about issues of cost and time and/or that screening could prevent parents from meeting in order to reach agreement. Only 14 per cent of family court officers ('court welfare officers' when the research was executed) appeared to be operating a 'safety-first' approach, across all aspects of their work, by interviewing both parties separately in order to ask questions about any fears or threats. The researchers conclude that mediators may need specialist training in order to develop their awareness of how violence might affect both the relationships between parents and also the mediation processes that take place. This is a need also recognised by Parkinson (1997, pp.258-9) who points out that:

> Practitioner members of the Academy of Family Mediators in the United States are required to have at least two hours of mediation training specifically on domestic violence issues.

Within the mediation session, seating patterns are variable although by far the most frequently reported configuration in the Essex study was 'face-to-face', that is the two parents are seated directly opposite each other. In fact, 87 per cent of participants in the research wrote that they had been seated in this potentially confrontational way: a small number wrote 'side-by-side' or described a 'triangular' arrangement between themselves, mediator and ex-partner. Of this 87 per cent, about seven out of ten had not found the arrangement a particular cause for concern. However, women were much more likely (about three times as likely, in fact) to have been concerned and described feelings of anxiety, worries about intimidation and having to make eye contact with their ex-partner. For many women, sitting directly opposite appeared to increase the sense of confrontation and feelings of being at risk, as the following set of quotations eloquently confirm:

My ex-husband is very intimidating. I try to have as little contact as possible with him as he has been abusive and threatening. Third parties have been used for contact transfers. It was difficult to face him and speak to him;

I found the seating arrangement very intimidating. This was the worst part of the session. I felt that my ex-husband could have reached across to me at any time;

It forces you to face the other person and was most unpleasant. Personally, I feel that we should both face the mediator;

I feel extremely intimidated by my ex-husband's presence and will avoid eye contact at all costs, partly due to incidents of domestic violence in the past but also I find his overall behaviour very threatening towards me.

It is illuminating to follow these narratives from women with a set of replies from men who had apparently preferred to be seated face-to-face with their ex-partners: a very different approach seems evident.

It didn't for me as I had no problem looking in the eyes of my ex- whereas she couldn't look at me;

I personally prefer direct confrontation;

I was very clever with my views and my ex-wife did not like that my views were being agreed with. This could be seen on her face which gave me the opportunity to sneer and give sarcastic grins. It sounds wrong but it made me feel wonderful.

Here the preoccupying concerns appear to be with ascendancy, conflict and the pursuit of 'psychological warfare', rather than the fear and anxiety portrayed by women participants. There were very few accounts from women that contained similar sentiments to those from men, although there were some, for example, '...it meant I could look him right in the eye when he was telling lies', and it is fair to say that, overall, the key concerns of women and men were markedly different in regard to the oppositional seating configuration used by mediators.

Violence *continues* in the mediation session, in the guises of trepidation, dominance and intimidation, but there is evidence that, occasionally, violence can *happen* immediately before, during or after mediation. Many women fear the possibility of violence but believe that the risk is lessened by the visibility of any attack to the other lay people and professionals present.

> Because of past abuse I find it frightening and intimidating to even be in the same room. The only comfort I find is that he must know he would be in serious trouble if he attacked me in a public place.

The incidents of violence reported by women in this context tend, understandably, to appear less serious in kind, although it is important to hold in mind the significance of such events within a history of violence in the relationship. Women in such circumstances, who are fearful and yet feel protected by the court setting and presence of officials, experience additional anxiety once the 'protection' begins to appear ineffective or insufficient – 'minor' events, such as the throwing of a pen or being pushed aside by their ex-partner (both incidents reported by women in the Essex study), can serve to call such social controls into question. As discussed in chapter 6, some women perceive a male mediator as an important provider of protection:

> The mediator was male and it was probably just as well as my ex-partner got very aggressive, loud and abusive and the mediator had to sort him out and I doubt my ex-partner would have taken any notice of a female.

Although most mediators appear to have used the confrontational approach in seating arrangements, a different configuration is apparent in about one in ten meetings: the two parties are here seated alongside one another thus avoiding obligatory eye-to-eye contact. However, there are also difficulties associated with this arrangement in that the parties may feel that the space between them is insufficient and, indeed, a small number of women in the study make reference to their unease and attempts to relieve it, 'Yes, I moved my chair from next to my ex-partner and put it next to my solicitor's the other side of the room'. Other women emphasised the difficulty of sharing a confined space with the other parent, whatever the seating pattern employed, 'I don't like having to be in the same room so it was difficult as he lies through his teeth and I find it frustrating to have to watch and listen to him', echoing the finding from research by Hester and Radford (1996) that many women are frightened or intimidated at having to share a room with their ex-partner.

Professional wisdom in this area of practice is quite clear: Liebmann (1998) outlines a seven-stage process for mediation developed for 'Mediation UK' (1995) – a charitable body comprising a network of projects, organisations and individuals interested in mediation – that advises mediators to seat the two parties comfortably '...so that they can see each other but are not directly facing each other' (p.47). Best practice, therefore, in this well-respected approach to mediation deliberately avoids the oppositional seating pattern that features so overwhelmingly in Essex county court family work.

Finally in this section it is important to acknowledge the jeopardy faced by the mediators themselves: in the course of their duties family court officers are also exposed to risks and the large-scale survey by Hester *et al.* (1997) reported that one in three officers had been verbally and/or physically abused by domestic violence perpetrators. Again, the conundrum of why family court officers continue to employ joint, and especially face-to-face mediation in cases where violence is possible or even likely must be raised.

## Violence, Intimidation and Male Power

> He intimidates me in unspoken ways which people can't pick up. He was sued for adultery because it's easier to prove than mental cruelty but that's what he should have been done for. Therefore, to sit in the same room shuts me up very fast.

As discussed earlier in this chapter, violence is most usefully conceptualised as a process rather than an event and, within such a conceptualisation, it is much easier to understand women's perception and experience of the abusive psychological aspects of their interactions with ex-partners such as bullying and browbeating. As 'violence' or as integral 'parts' of violence, the seriousness of their impact may more readily be sensed. The above words from a woman participant in the Essex study serve to draw attention to the 'hidden' quality of intimidation – it is not always easy to detect – and highlight the effect that such intimidatory tactics may have on women's ability to articulate their case during mediation. Many contemporary definitions of 'domestic violence' incorporate both physical and mental abuse: the Association of Chief Officers of Probation (1996), for example, has published a position statement that area probation services are following which defines domestic violence as:

> ...men's violence toward women, behaviour which is deliberate and conscious abuse of male power to control women in relationships and the

home, forming part of a continuum which ranges through threats and intimidation to sexual abuse, rape and murder (in Ashworth, 1997, p.140).

but, as can be seen, such definitions also often limit the meaning of domestic violence, restricting its currency to male activity, and linking it to the abuse of male power and to male heterosexuality. There is considerable debate around this issue (Dixon, 1998), the essence of the counter argument being that domestic violence is a much more complex phenomenon, one that requires a multi-dimensional explanatory framework. However, the findings of the Essex study would seem to suggest that definitions which highlight male attempts to intimidate and dominate might be the more apposite. Certainly, there is a great deal of evidence supporting the view that women are much more likely to feel intimidated and disempowered during mediation sessions and, furthermore, that women's feelings of unease and lack of confidence are closely associated with male violence. Many women 'freeze' during mediation; in other words the combination of formality, associated with attendance at court, alongside concerns about their ex-partner makes it very difficult for women to give of their best.

A broad conceptualisation of 'violence' or 'abuse', incorporating psychological, economic and physical dimensions, has many advantages but, as might be expected, there are disadvantages too. Most significant is the potential for losing sight of the serious instances of physical assault that do occur. In the mediation context, this may result in complacency and it is important for all those concerned with the management and delivery of mediation services to recognise the risk of serious injury that some women will face. Research is patchy in this area and, although there are some references to the issue in the literature, much more needs to be done. Stelman (1993, p.197) refers to the murder of Vandana Patel by her estranged husband in 1991. Hester and Radford (1996, p.31) describe a number of cases from their research:

> One welfare officer expressed concern that a woman he may have encouraged to attend a joint meeting had been stabbed by her ex-partner in front of her children as she left the court welfare offices. Another expressed regret that he may have engendered a false sense of security in a woman whom he had encouraged to face a violent partner in a joint meeting. After the meeting the man telephoned the woman and asked if he could come to the house to collect the children for a contact visit. She consented and he axed her to death on the doorstep. The killing was witnessed by her children. Welfare officers interviewed told us of three other domestic

homicides of women which they felt had been linked to the court welfare services' involvement in contact cases.

The same authors also refer to one joint mediation meeting at which the woman was beaten by her ex-partner despite the fact that the meeting was being video-taped. In their major study of voluntary sector mediation, McCarthy and Walker (1996, p.41) make only passing reference to the issue of domestic violence in the mediation context: the authors quote the following words from one woman who had suffered at the hands of her ex-partner:

> My ex-husband was a violent man at home but gave the outward look of the victim in all of this. However, twice after mediation appointments, he attacked me outside. Despite my pleas they always insisted on us leaving together, or him leaving first.

A further difficulty ensuing from a broad definition of violence is the tendency to lose sight of the fact that perpetration, both in terms of prevalence and severity, is essentially a male preserve. If 'violence', as a category, is defined so as to include both psychological and physical abuse then, of course, men may be equally as likely to be 'violent' as women. The problem with this 'tendency to parity' is twofold: first, men, in addition to employing emotional bullying, are much more likely to be physically violent, and to use more serious violence than women; and, second, the threat of physical attack changes the very nature and intensity of the *process* of psychological abuse, so that, in this vital sense, there is no ready equivalence between the sexes. This is not to say that men are never abused by women, rather that the abuse perpetrated by men should be the major focus of those with a responsibility for the management or delivery of mediation services. Some writers have, perhaps, over-reacted to such a position: Parkinson (1997, p.254), for example, opines that:

> Members of the 'helping professions' may be more sensitive to women being victims and may antagonise men by labelling them as violent without enquiring carefully enough. They may also covertly discourage a man from admitting that he has been abused by a woman because this is more shameful for a man to admit.

On the two points made: first, the 'antagonism' of men would appear to be a price worth paying in the interests of identifying violence;

and, second, women are also ashamed that they have been obliged to suffer violence.

Closely related to a broad notion of violence is a contemporary enthusiasm for the idea that people can be *both* perpetrators and survivors. In turn, this idea might be linked to the voluntarism-determinism divide within criminology (Young, 1981, pp.250–1) and more recent attempts to develop a constitutive or affirmative, rather than a sceptical, position in that field of study, policy and practice (Henry and Milovanovic, 1996, pp.16–44). Stanko (1998, p.52) puts it thus:

> In order to confront the insidious portrayal of women as blameworthy for the violence of men...much of the work exploring the victimisation of women emphasized the impact of gendered oppression as a significant contributor to women's subordination...At the same time, women's offending was explored for its active agency...The dilemma for theorists, however, is to reconcile the notion of agency with the dynamics of structured oppression. Why is it so difficult for us in criminology to accept that women and men can be both victims and offenders?...What are the overlaps, and where does offending/victimization not overlap?

A comprehensive response to such questions posed is well beyond the brief of this book, although it might be helpful at this point to say that, at least within the area of 'domestic violence', there appear to be: (1) substantial differences in male and female patterns of activity, providing evidence for the view that 'structured oppression', to use Stanko's terminology, remains firmly established; and (2) many more gaps than overlaps, in terms of offending/victimisation.

In summary, there are grounds to suggest that women are exposed to the risk of violent incidents before, during and after mediation meetings. In a minority of cases such incidents will be very serious indeed, resulting in death or serious injury and associated psychological trauma. However, there will be many more violent events of a less serious nature that, nevertheless, cause injury and/or distress. It is therefore incumbent upon all court personnel to ensure an acceptable level of safety and, in cases where the woman cannot be protected, mediation should not be attempted.

Sharing a waiting area, then sharing a much smaller space with one's assailant in order to seek agreement look to be risky and demanding hurdles for any woman to overcome. Being obliged to sit directly opposite that person, in confrontational mode, appears even more hazardous and it is difficult to imagine how such practice might be given any professional value. In attempting to understand why most family court officers appear to favour this approach, there are grounds to suggest that many officers are insufficiently aware both of the prevalence of violence and of the effects of violence upon women undergoing joint mediation meetings. The effect of years of violence upon a woman's self-esteem (Dowling and Gorell Barnes, 2000, p.115) is likely to be particularly significant:

> Work with women often many years after they have left a violent context, suggests that even though a woman may have accepted that violence itself is unacceptable, the effect of years of living in a system organised about the possibility of violent behaviour erupting has long-lasting effects on a sense of security and of self-esteem.

It is also important to appreciate the unpredicted ramifications of a central tenet of mediation practice. Mediators attempt to shift attention away from the past, to help the two parties look to how they might jointly manage their affairs concerning their child/children in the future. 'Relationship abuse', on the other hand, refers to a long-term phenomenon, incorporating both past incidents of assault and abuse, and processual responses to such events or longer periods when survival and maintaining a level of self-respect had been uppermost on the woman's agenda. On the basis of their interviews with court welfare officers, Hester and Radford (1996, p.15) conclude that:

> ...domestic violence was viewed as a problem of the 'past' relationship, and no longer relevant to the current situation. Women were castigated for dredging up incidents of domestic violence which had happened in the past because they were 'hurt' or hoping to gain an advantage in contact or residency applications.

The authors describe how even very serious examples of violence had been minimised by court officers, apparently because of the prevailing principle that parties should be encouraged to focus solely on the 'future'. Such practice would seem to be misguided, based as it is upon a simplistic conceptualisation of violence and its effects.

Mediators also attempt to be 'even-handed' in their practice, to allow equal time to both parties to have their say, but this may simply serve to conceal steep differences in power, confidence and opportunity. In cases where the relationship continues to be abusive, such attempts at parity would seem especially questionable and it would not be unreasonable to suggest that some form of advocacy might be more appropriate (Liebmann, 1998, p.50).

There are three further factors that may play a part. First, there is evidence of a culture of 'individualism' amongst family court personnel, in which emphasis and worth are attributed to the different styles that officers possess – so, the confrontational, 'eyeball-to eyeball' mode becomes just another style or personal preference and its employment may be justified as such. Ashworth (1995, p.93) links this phenomenon to a lack of rigorous evaluation:

> It is generally accepted that family court welfare work is a neglected area of probation activity and is grossly under-researched. In addition, there exist wide variations in practice, supported by competing professional arguments, but with little or no qualitative analysis.

Second, the probation service, of which the family court service is a part, has over the past decades been encouraged by successive governments to 'confront' offenders, to talk tough, to switch from a 'welfare' to a 'control' agency, from social service to law enforcement and it is possible that the confrontation mode has gained some support within this broader milieu. Third, the pressure to reach an 'agreement', or have the court decide, may encourage some mediators to 'go for broke', to 'knock heads together' (Parkinson, 1997, p.70), or, in Heron's (1977) terminology to employ a 'nutcracker' form of intervention, all of which can be linked with the use of a seating arrangement that obliges parents to have eye contact and to speak directly to each other. The location of family court work is being changed and this would appear to be a logical and desirable move given the emergent philosophy of the contemporary probation service, or 'community punishment and rehabilitation service'.

Finally, it is possible to cite the dearth of research and related paucity in theoretical resources as key factors in understanding why the identification and appraisal of intimate partner violence continues to be low priority for mediators. As outlined in chapter 2, there are conceptual frameworks that appear to present potentially fruitful opportunities for application and development within the mediation field. The three parenting approaches offered by Maccoby *et al.* (1990), for example, may be worthy of general exploration within mediation practice and there would certainly appear to be value in testing how useful the notions of 'co-operative, conflicted and disengaged' might prove to be in attempts to identify and manage partner violence in mediation. It might reasonably be predicted that mediators would focus primarily upon the 'conflicted' pattern of parenting as more likely to be associated with violence, given the ongoing acrimony and emotional tension manifested. Less attention might therefore be afforded to 'disengaged' parents – that is, where communication only takes place via the child or children – and this might obscure the risk of violence in such cases. After all, parents who have spent months or years avoiding direct contact, thereby making conflict less likely, may experience highly-charged and unpredictable reactions when they finally come to share an enclosed space in the context of an expectation that they do communicate directly.

**Summary**

The establishment of 'new language' looks to be a priority in future discourse within this field. The notion of 'domestic violence' carries too much baggage from centuries of mollification, while 'separation' and 'violence', as discrete terms and in combination, suggest incidents or events, rather than on-going processes. Although it is recognised that an ideal terminology is unlikely to exist, there may be opportunities for improvement and the precision and utility of 'intimate partner violence' and 'separation violence' appear to be worthy of further consideration.

Changing policy and practice in family court mediation appears to be slow-moving. Certainly, the lead from central government could have been much more directly focused and the absence of any guidance in national standards appears to be particularly remiss. On the other hand, there is evidence to suggest that, even where central policy is clear, local policies and practices may be stubbornly resistant to change. Practitioners, managers and governors must all bear a responsibility for this state of affairs but it is also important to recognise the wider constraints of limited finance and of dependence on the availability and quality of court-based accommodation and access to legal and judicial personnel. At county court, family court officers practise in an environment that is not their own and, within which, they have restricted powers. The priority they award to the issue of partner violence must, to some extent, be shaped by the strength of competing claims, such as the widespread and legitimised presumption that contact between the child and non-resident father is (almost) always desirable. Similarly, the views and attitudes of other court personnel will play an important part and there is some evidence to suggest that many judges may still respond with indifference or impatience to abused women (Ptacek, 1999).

The tripartite relationships between intimate partner violence, the likelihood of parties reaching agreement during mediation, and the durability of agreements look to be eminently worthy of further research. The question of how the 'settlement rate' (Walker *et al.*, 1994, p.71) might behave according to the incidence of violence is an intriguing one and provisional answers to it would undoubtedly be of enormous value. If it is possible to say that mediators may currently press ahead with unsafe cases on the grounds of a belief that settlement is achievable, then research evidence on the robustness of those 'agreements' over time would be very important in moves to encourage mediators towards safer practice.

There is no little irony in conciliatory interventions currently taking place within the confines of county courts, given their close associations with justice and protection. Many women face intimidation and are frightened that their abusive relationships may again flare up into assault. That this should not only be allowed to happen but largely remain unacknowledged and, in effect, be exacerbated through the sharing of waiting areas and use of confrontational seating arrangements during mediation, appears highly questionable, if not impossible to justify. These are practices ripe for review and change, and call into question other family court procedures that fail to operate on the foundation of 'safety-first' principles. The establishment of services that are sensitive to women's experiences of separation and violence would appear to be a priority for the new, unified agency to pursue. The final words of this chapter belong to a woman participant in the Essex study: they express well-worn sentiments that not only call for further, sustained efforts on the part of all those concerned with family court work but also support the conclusion of this chapter that 'domestic' still implies 'less serious'.

> Violence in the home is still treated very much as a domestic problem and not as a serious issue.

# 5 Solicitors, District Judges and Courtrooms

This chapter considers mediation within its legal-judicial context and, more specifically, critically examines the ways in which the involvement of lawyers and judges may shape the processes, experiences and outcomes of mediation for parents. County court mediation takes place primarily on court premises, district judges are directly informed of the outcome and substance of the mediation meeting, and solicitors are more often than not present during mediation. These are powerful factors and, although their respective effects are certainly contested in the albeit, limited literature, the need for their inclusion within this account of mediation is clear.

Support, information and advice for parents are all likely to be at a premium during separation and divorce, and sources will include not only court-based services but also lawyers, teachers and family doctors. Cockett and Tripp's (1994) study in Exeter found that parents were especially likely to consult such professionals at this time and the 'gate keeping' role of, particularly, solicitors in divorce and related procedures is firmly established. It follows, therefore, that solicitors are likely to play a key part in referring parents to mediation services. Furthermore, there may be two main ways in which they may affect mediation: first, in terms of the proportion of cases referred; and, second, in terms of the 'messages' about mediation that parents may pick up from solicitors. If, as Davis (1999, p.633) argues, many solicitors are unhappy about new procedures – especially where they feel obliged to refer cases they consider to be unsuitable – then there must be repercussions for how they present mediation to parents. If this is done 'grudgingly', rather than in a more balanced or positive way, parents may have their expectations and understanding of mediation significantly diminished. Interest in the gate keeping relationship between legal services and mediation has been significantly enhanced by the arrival and continuing implementation of section 29 of the *Family Law Act, 1996*. Section 29 amends section 15 of the *Legal Aid Act 1988* to the effect that anyone pursuing legal representation for the purposes of proceedings relating to family matters must attend a meeting with a mediator in order first to determine the suitability of mediation and, second, to assist the person applying for representation to apply instead for mediation. Needless to say the response to s.29 has been mixed: many solicitors have been concerned about the delays produced and by the apparent rigidities in the operation of s.29, and this chapter includes an account charting the solicitors' perspective through the consultative preparations for the *Family Law Act*. At this point in writing, it is perhaps sufficient to say that the Legal Aid Board Mediation Pilot scheme has continued to develop and that, nationally, only some 22 per cent of 'suitability meetings' convert to mediation (Nichols, 1999, p.657).

Having established the significance of the gate keeping function carried out by solicitors, it is also important to acknowledge the longer-term work that lawyers undertake with divorcing and divorced couples. As already mentioned, parents attending county court mediation are normally accompanied by their respective legal representative and contact often continues for some time after mediation. One way of conceptualising this interconnection is, in fact, to regard the relationship between mediation and legal 'representation' as mutually helpful and, perhaps, even necessary for effective practice. Nichols (1999, p.657), for example, goes as far as opining that:

> Mediation works for the benefit of clients only when practised hand in hand with good legal advice, before, during and after the mediation process. Mediation without legal advice is a blind guide which will only lead others, along with itself, into a ditch,

while Parkinson (1997, p.3) questions the very notion of mediation as a substitute for legal processes. Of course, this insistence on complementarity rather than opposition produces its own theoretical problems – after all, a manageable amount of conflict or tension is rarely a bad thing and may usefully serve to maintain a healthy discussion of a broad range of pertinent issues. Questions of welfare and justice, for example, are frequently uneasy stable-mates and yet both are necessary considerations within the context of divorce. Furthermore, execution of the lawyer's role in this domain itself has to encompass the need for both 'aggressive representation and the sustenance of interdependent family relationships after the legal process is completed' (Kline Pruett and Jackson, 1999, p.287). In other words, the task is multi-faceted, rather than simple, and likely to involve a number of dilemmas and mutually contrary elements. Effective practice, for mediators and lawyers, may therefore require the maintenance of some measure of internal and external dissonance, uncomfortable as that may be.


## The Lawyer's Role During Mediation

Although many lawyers now act as mediators (Parkinson, 1997, pp.78–9), this discussion is concerned with the role of solicitors who accompany their clients to mediation sessions facilitated by one or more family court officer. The vast majority of divorcing parents who undergo mediation are legally represented and it is common practice for solicitors to be present during mediation. As Walker *et al.* (1994, p.131) point out, the expectation to engage a lawyer has been strongest in the case of comprehensive or all issues mediation, mainly because of the particular expertise that solicitors possess in regard to financial matters. Nevertheless, county court, child-focused mediation also characteristically involves the attendance of solicitors – the mediation ensemble thus usually consists of five people, six if there are two mediators present. Mediation cannot therefore be fully understood nor adequately analysed as a meeting of two parties in dispute, facilitated by a professional mediator – each parent normally has their respective legal 'representative' sitting close by and, although solicitors may play little active part in the mediation discussions, their presence and availability for consultation are nonetheless important factors. Whether their involvement is beneficial is, of course, open to question but it is not possible to ignore the role that they currently undertake.

Two ready concerns about the presence of solicitors during mediation are first that an undue dependency may be encouraged and second that an unhelpful, adversarial approach or mood may be produced. It has been recognised for some time that not to engage the services of a solicitor may be hazardous (Davis, 1988, p.14), which perhaps suggests that some parents may become over-dependent on their legal adviser. More generally, a view has developed that, because divorcing parents often experience a lessened feeling of 'being in control', as routine patterns of life disappear, the exposure to a powerful and unpredictable legal system may produce an even greater sense of helplessness. In such circumstances, a dependency on the legal experts may result. Similarly, the arrival and spread of mediation has, at least in part, been driven by a desire to move away from the traditionally adversarial mode adopted by lawyers. Mediation is one manifestation of 'ADR', or 'Alternative Dispute Resolution', and the 'alternative' in question is usually perceived to be litigation. There is little research evidence on the question of over-dependency but there are some empirical findings to support the contention that solicitors may exacerbate the level of conflict between parents: Walker *et al.* (1994), for example, asked users of mediation services to rate the extent to which they had been helped in settling their disagreements by a range of professionals and found that, while 23 per cent of users suggested that their own solicitor had reduced conflict (compared to 19 per cent who increased it), 57 per cent believed that their ex-partner's solicitor had made matters worse. In sharp contrast, 50 per cent of mediation users said that mediators had reduced the level of antagonism (p.129). It would be possible therefore to suggest that mediators and solicitors adopt very different approaches in addressing disputes and, furthermore, that some degree of tension may consequently arise between the two professions.

Some research studies have attempted to compare and contrast mediation and litigation in terms of, *inter alia*, the effects on the level of parent to parent conflict. Kelly (1991) found that mediation was associated with less conflict, more communication and a more positive attitude toward the other party up to two years after the settlement. Similar results have been reported by Dillon and Emery (1996). However, there is certainly no consensus on this question and Davis (1999) is able to conclude that, although there is a widely held view that lawyers do amplify antagonism, the view is not supported by the research evidence.

In the Essex study, three quarters of parents had been legally represented and a similar proportion (74 per cent) had felt that the presence of solicitors at the mediation meeting had been beneficial, in line with the findings of earlier, more general research concerned with the views of parents (Davis, 1999, p.626). Where the presence of solicitors had been regarded as helpful, the availability of immediate legal/procedural advice emerges as a major theme in the replies:

> Although my solicitor was not allowed to interfere in the discussions, there were legal issues that I needed advice on there and then.
>
> I was incredibly nervous, ex-husband is hardly friendly. It was helpful to have someone to ask for breaks, remind me of things I totally forgot (due to fear).

Similarly, the 'support' provided by solicitors was important in many cases, as was the role of the solicitor in recalling what had been discussed and agreed. Other themes include the enhanced sense of significance, gravity and orderliness of the session and the opportunity for lawyers to observe the shortcomings of the 'other' parent.

Not surprisingly the supportive role played by lawyers during mediation has a number of dimensions and is demonstrated in a range of different ways. Most often, support was used as a buffer between the two parents: sometimes there were explicit references to the need for protection from the 'other' parent:

> My ex-husband is a person who can argue well, using impressive words. He has been physically and verbally abusive to me. The presence of my solicitor gave me support and confidence,

and there were cases where solicitors had taken a more active role because of intimidation:

> My solicitor had to speak on my behalf in the end as I got very upset and did not want to speak to my ex-partner who was being rude and abusive.

Interestingly, some parents described a need for such active support in relation to the mediator rather than the other parent:

> Our solicitor took a lot of pressure off us. I feel the social worker (*sic*) there was much too pushy and my solicitor stepped in.

> The mediator was not prepared to listen to me fully and it was up to my solicitor to make my point heard.

One Essex study mother had a very special reason for valuing her solicitor's presence:

> I suffer from depression mostly resulting from my ex's behaviour. To be on my own with him I could not do and I would have had to have a GP's letter to bring someone in with me. Having a solicitor meant that the mediators needn't know about my depression and also meant someone was there for me,

a testimony that raises a number of questions about how individuals who feel vulnerable may avoid disclosure and about mediator sensitivities and practices in this context.

However, the involvement of legal advisers was not universally welcomed and, in responses indicating that the presence of solicitors had not been helpful, there were three prominent themes: first, some parents referred directly to the negative effects of the adversarial mode adopted by solicitors:

> My ex-wife's solicitor always disagreed with what was agreed making it more of a fight between my solicitor and her solicitor,

while others felt that having lawyers present during mediation produced a dramaturgical side to proceedings in which parties felt obliged to present in a less than authentic fashion:

> Well, when me and my wife do speak we get on nearly fine but in court and with solicitors she has to keep up hostilities in front of an audience to be convincing so her solicitor believes her,

and, third, the involvement of solicitors was seen by some as detracting from the need for parents to sort things out for themselves and their children:

> I feel that it is in the best interests of the child/children that the parent tries to reach an agreement, both financially and emotionally, without the need for solicitors.

In addition, a small number of Essex study parents had evidently expected that their adviser would play a much more active part during mediation:

> I thought the solicitor would do all the talking. I was surprised I had to almost talk directly with my ex- and this was uncomfortable because he had been violent previously,

which gives a new twist to the issue of whether or not the presence of solicitors may encourage an over-dependency in parents. In this case the woman had evidently felt unready for such close interaction with her previously abusive ex-partner and, in such circumstances, it would not be unreasonable to expect a greater degree of advocacy from her legal representative, even if this might be construed as disempowering in the longer term.

Also, there was a small number of complaints about particular aspects of the solicitor's performance, including poor time-keeping and not providing sufficient preparatory information for the mediation meeting:

He failed to turn up on time, delayed the session and wasn't allowed any input anyway.

My solicitor did not tell me what was going to happen on that day nor was I told anything by the mediator prior to the hearing.

Broadly, it is fair to say that Essex study parents were either in favour or against the presence of solicitors during mediation meetings, although the questionnaire design no doubt encouraged this polarity to a considerable extent. Nevertheless, there was a handful of responses that demonstrated a more ambivalent position and there may be grounds to believe that such ambivalence was more commonplace than the study findings suggest. Certainly, there is evidence to support a view that, overall, parents are indeed uncertain and circumspect about the role of lawyers in divorce: Sarat and Felstiner (1986, p.129), for example, argue that such ambivalence may be expressed by parents resisting the advice and proposals that the lawyer regards as clearly in the client's interest.

The value of the 'supportive' role played by solicitors should not be underestimated. Understandably, parents who are divorcing or separating are likely to be distressed and struggling to cope in a rational manner and there is ample research evidence to suggest that this is indeed the case (Mitchell, 1985; Rodgers and Pryor, 1998, p.45). There are many adjustments for them to make and having the ongoing support and advice from someone who has relevant experience and expertise obviously counts for a great deal. It is also important to recognise that the two parents may be at different stages of adjustment – the party who first left the marriage may have come to terms with the separation, while the other may still be overwhelmed by feelings of loss or betrayal – and therefore that the need for support may also be different. Parkinson (1997, p.39) argues that couples who come to mediation may be categorised as '...those who are able to talk and work things out, those who argue and fight, and those who cannot talk at all', and it may be useful to consider both the need for legal representatives and the function(s) they might best perform against this analytical frame. The same author opines that mediators should be able to adapt their approach according to the stage in the separation that each parent has reached: solicitors, then, may require a similar sensitivity. Finally, it is important to recall the violence and abuse reported by a significant proportion of women in the Essex study and, indeed, by participants in many other research projects in this field: in such circumstances, the support and protection provided by legal representatives is regarded as essential by many women.

## Mediation Without Legal Representation

Perhaps one quarter of parents who attend county court mediation do so without legal representation and, given the widespread belief that to undergo divorce without a lawyer is not to be lightly recommended, there is much to commend an especial focus on the experiences and views of this group. Certainly, there is evidence from a broader canvas that such experiences may often be difficult, particularly when the other party is legally supported. Research by Yegge (1994), for example, found that, although '*pro se*' litigants were as satisfied with the terms of their decrees as those who had been represented, more satisfied with the legal process and more satisfied with judges than attorney-represented litigants, only 36 per cent of *pro se* respondents who faced represented petitioners said that they would proceed without a lawyer again, while 79 per cent of attorney represented petitioners would proceed with a lawyer again (p.410). In other words, many of those individuals who had been exposed to legal expertise wielded on behalf of their ex-partner would not wish to repeat the experience.

In the Essex study, the main reasons given for not having a solicitor at mediation were the expense and a belief that lawyers were unnecessary or that they might even detract from the need to reach agreement:

> If you are confident on your own, why consider paying for costly solicitor fees? If there were 'free of charge services' available I probably would have accepted.

> My ex- and I felt we could reach agreement anyway.

> They feed the fight and don't help.

> Any contact with solicitors of any description is a process which impoverishes not only one's heart and soul but also one's pocket

and, for a few parents, there was also a suspicion about the solicitor's primary motivation, 'I believe it is a personal experience which solicitors would use to their own ends, solutions are bad for business!'

Some Essex study parents had evidently regretted their decision not to employ a legal representative because they had felt unsupported and/or they had missed the lawyer's role of keeping a record of the mediation agreement:

On previous sessions I have had a solicitor present, it gave me confidence and I also had some form of written evidence of the agreement,

while others said that they had not been able to afford a solicitor even though they wanted to be represented:

I never had a solicitor because of the expense, my ex-wife did because she was able to get legal aid. This placed me at a disadvantage – I feel no solicitors should be present at all.

Some unrepresented parents reported unhelpful interventions by their ex-partner's solicitor:

The fact that her solicitor took me into a room and tried to get me to agree to only having contact with my son for one and a half hours a week, which I refused,

and others made reference to the adversarial atmosphere created:

The Children Act is supposed to be non-adversarial but in my experience it clearly is. I had to attend the hearing and be told by the father's barrister that he was there to represent my daughter. Luckily I am fairly strong and articulate but I dread to think how a vulnerable person would cope without representation.

In concluding this section there is a need to focus sharply on the cost of legal representation to parents who are in the process of divorce. If, as it would appear, some parents who are ineligible for legal aid feel unable to afford a lawyer then mediators must be aware of the possible repercussions for the quality and dynamics of the mediation meeting. Furthermore, it is clear that the financial cost of employing a solicitor may continue for years after mediation has taken place and that the sums involved are likely to place a heavy burden on anyone of average or below average income. The Essex study data offers many examples of parents who continue to use a solicitor in order to facilitate the terms of the mediation agreement, for instance:

They said at the meeting we would *have* [original emphasis] to compromise on what dates were suitable but with my ex-husband there is no compromise. He is being totally unreasonable and making it very difficult about any times I would like to see my children. What was the point in the mediation if afterwards I keep having to pay my solicitor to sort out dates? The costs have already totalled £4,000,

a testimony that is contributed by a mother who, in spite of the further difficulties and heavy expense, had felt that her settlement was still intact six months after the mediation meeting.

Concerns about the financial aspects of mediation are, of course, nothing new and the accepted wisdom has for some time been that child-focused mediation is likely to involve higher expenditure. In the Newcastle study McCarthy and Walker (1996) reported that, while 44 per cent of users of all-issues mediation had felt that mediation had helped them obtain a cheaper divorce, only 13 per cent of users of child-focused mediation suggested that this had been the case. Similarly, the earlier study of child-focused conciliation by the Conciliation Project Unit (1989) concluded that, overall, 'mediation' adds to, rather than subtracts from, the cost of divorce. However, it is acknowledged that, at time of writing, the effects of a number of significant changes in the relationship between legal services and mediation remain unclear. The respective arrivals and activities of the Community Legal Service and the Legal Services Commission are having important repercussions for policy and practice in this arena, while the Legal Aid Board's report to the Lord Chancellor's Department at completion of the national mediation pilot scheme is keenly awaited. The current environment is one of considerable flux and uncertainty. Clerke (2000, pp.574–5) points out that legal advice before mediation is provided under simple 'legal help' while advice during and after mediation is now defined as 'help with mediation' and is only available if the client is either involved in mediation or has already reached a mediated agreement. Solicitors may therefore be employed for advice during mediation and for assistance in putting the settlement into effect. However, the financial limits imposed, of £150 for child-focused, £250 for finance-only, and £350 for all issues cases, would appear to be particularly austere.

**What do Lawyers Think About Mediation?**

As already pointed out in this chapter, some solicitors provide mediation themselves and the occurrence of 'solicitor mediators' needs to be recognised in responding to the question of how lawyers perceive mediation. The combination of roles was traditionally seen as untenable, especially because of the likely conflicts of interest when working with both parties, but the practice has recently achieved official recognition in the form of a code of practice for family mediation (Law Society of England and Wales, 1997), which is addressed to solicitors who mediate in family disputes. In the USA, the American Bar Association passed the 'Model Rules of Mediation for Attorneys' in 1984 and various 'codes of ethics' have been established by family law groups – see Moore (1996) and Loeb (1999) for accounts of these developments.

Notwithstanding the phenomenon of the solicitor mediator, the two professional arenas are eminently distinguishable and so the search for what lawyers think about mediation remains a useful and valid exercise. On the basis of two recent consultation surveys, McCarthy (2000, p.553) concludes that, although members of the legal profession are not as enthusiastic about mediation as are other 'divorce-associated' professionals – counsellors, mediators and family court officers, there is reason to believe that many lawyers have now accepted its viability in dispute resolution. This is an important finding, not least because it alerts us to the long-standing tensions between mediation and legal practice. In order to comprehend present-day circumstances, it is necessary to take an historical view, tracing the development of mediation services within and beyond the castle walls of an already established and powerful profession.

Cretney (2000, p.68) reminds us that the divorce process has traditionally been choreographed by solicitors, with each party employing their own lawyer and rules of professional conduct intended to avoid conflict of interest, meaning that solicitors were prevented from acting for both husband and wife. By contrast, of course, mediators do work with both parties and this marks an important and long-standing distinction between the two forms of professional engagement. The notion of working with both parties and, in particular, the prospect of face to face meetings with both parties, must have seemed rather strange, possibly dangerous, to solicitors in the early days of conciliation, since renamed 'mediation'. Similarly, conciliators and, subsequently, mediators would no doubt have been highly suspicious of the traditional mode operated by lawyers, regarding it as likely to exacerbate conflict between parents. The term 'adversarial' came to carry unfortunate implications within the context of divorce, in spite of the fragility of empirical evidence one way or the other. Kline Pruett and Jackson (1999, p.286) conclude that, although there is some support for the view that litigation worsens the already antagonistic dynamics during separation and divorce, little is known about what happens during the legal process to support or undermine the successful adaptation of children and parents. Nevertheless, the opinion that litigation was both inappropriate and financially costly came to ascendancy and conciliation was presented as a preferable option on both counts. In the USA, conciliation was described as the 'better way' during the 1980s following an influential article by Chief Justice Warren Burger (1982) entitled 'Isn't There a Better Way?'.

The rising rate of marital breakdown, during the late 1960s and early 1970s, and specific concerns about the effects of divorce on children are usually cited as reasons for the arrival and growth of conciliation services, while *The Finer Committee Report* (1974) provided an early informed declaration in favour of conciliation. Government, however, was slow to grant any official support and it was therefore left to devotees from a range of professional backgrounds – social workers, probation officers, counsellors and lawyers – to develop the use of conciliation within the context of divorce and separation. As might be expected from such origins, conciliation services were initially less than uniform and, in fact, soon bifurcated, with one branch being provided by area probation services and the other by voluntary agencies. The first voluntary service was set up in Bristol in 1978, although the involvement of probation officers in conciliation certainly began much earlier. Bretherton (1979, p.75), for example, writes that the court welfare officer has three main tasks: first, collecting information for the purpose of writing a report for the court; second, to conciliate; and, third, to act as a counsellor for either or both parents or the child/children. By the late 1970s conciliation was already an established part of mainstream court welfare practice, although there were and, indeed, still are significant variations from one probation service area to another.

Given this rather irregular pattern of development, the attitudes of lawyers towards and, indeed, their levels of knowledge about mediation were understandably varied. Relatedly, levels of interest, involvement and resistance were no doubt also wide-ranging across the country, depending upon the particularities of local developments and inter-professional understandings. In the absence of official sanction from government, the likelihood is that most lawyers were cautious with, perhaps, the closest affinity being to the statutory, and hence legitimised, work executed by probation service court welfare workers. This is not to discount the early work of (small numbers of) lawyers in conciliation, then mediation work, offered by the voluntary sector: the intention is to seek a broader picture on which to set the next important shift in practice, from a child-focused to a comprehensive mode of working. In 1988, lawyers and mediators set up the Family Mediators Association which championed the advantages of all-issues mediation over its child-centred sibling. The 'better way' – mediation – had thus produced its own internal rank order, with comprehensive mediation taking the higher position.

The consultation period leading up to the arrival of the *Family Law Act 1996* provides a wealth of critical commentary concerned with mediation and, indeed, with other provisions within the legislation. The Act presents mediation as a central component of the new divorce proceedings and, because of this emphasis and underpinning conviction, it is not surprising that criticisms were both profound and legion. The Law Commission (1990) had advocated the use of mediation, while acknowledging the risk of relying too heavily upon it, with respect to the more traditional methods of negotiation and adjudication (para. 5.34). The Commission identified three key dangers: first, the possible exploitation of one parent by the other; second, a considerable potential for delay which could be damaging to the interests of the children and often to one of the adults involved; and, third, a temptation for the court to postpone difficult decisions that ought to be taken as quickly as possible. Nevertheless, the government maintained its commitment to mediation in both Green and White Papers, published in 1993 and 1995 respectively, on the heels of which followed the 1996 Act. Freeman (1996, p.38) summarises, within a brief review of the literature, the many grounds for concern expressed by academics and lawyers while Cretney (2000, pp.79–82) presents three major criticisms of the Act: (1) that there may, with some irony given the aims of the legislation, be created a host of additional opportunities for adversarial litigation; (2) that the expectations for mediation within the 1996 Act are much too ambitious; and (3) that the law is founded upon unrealistic assumptions about the needs and likely reactions of human beings involved in the painful processes of separation and divorce. The second of these three concerns is clearly worthy of further consideration here. Cretney registers the widespread anxiety over resourcing, citing the reluctance on the part of successive governments to fund mediation. The lack of adequately trained mediators, over-reliance on the voluntary sector coupled with the decision to defer implementation of the 1996 Act are identified as key reasons for concern connected with the issue of funding. Even where mediators have received training, a good number quickly lose their skills through lack of practice experience – Walker and Hornick (1996), for example, found that 19 per cent of FMA trained mediators had not practised for two or more years after qualification. Closely related is the continuing worry about professional competence, especially in regard to the view that mediation may exploit the more vulnerable parent. While acknowledging the standard-setting initiatives carried out by the United Kingdom College of Family Mediators – established in 1996 by the three organisations, Family Mediators Association, Family Mediation Scotland and National Family Mediation – Cretney rightly argues that there is, as yet, no means of ensuring compliance with the codes of conduct and standards of competence devised. Similar concerns are evident in the United States: Loeb (1999), for example, identifies codes of ethics designed and promoted by the Academy of Family Mediators, the Association of Family and Conciliation Courts and the Society of Professionals in Dispute Resolution. The situation is further complicated by the existence of alternative training pathways for family lawyers who wish to mediate (see Parkinson, 1997, pp.357–9). Finally, Cretney questions the view, expounded by both Labour and Conservative governments, that mediation would be perceived by parents considering divorce as an attractive and effective option. There is certainly evidence to suggest that the widely quoted words from the Legal Aid Board (1996) that '40 per cent of family cases in the future could involve mediation' (p.18) reflected an unrealistic ambition and the author suggests that fewer than one in ten actually opt for mediation. The arrival of section 29 referrals has done little to change this picture: Davis (1999, p.631), for example, states that,

> Prior to the introduction of s.29 the number of mediation starts was around seven cases per month among not-for-profit services and one case per month among for profit services. Following s.29, the mean is of the order of 10 cases per month (not-for-profit suppliers) and 2.5 cases per month (for profit suppliers).

Of course, it is also necessary to show that, in cases where mediation is chosen, a satisfactory rate of settlements is achieved and that, as argued in chapter 2, a reasonable proportion of the agreements stand the test of time. On this latter point, solicitors may experience some difficulty in gaining a balanced view because, as a matter of course, they are more likely to become aware of the settlements that have not persisted, as parents return for further, often remedial, advice. In turn this may feed their anxieties about referring 'high risk' cases, for whom mediation may be inappropriate. There is a long-standing belief among lawyers that mediation may be offered prematurely to parents who are too traumatised to respond to its demands: Bryan (1994, pp.207-08) opines that,

The lawyer's first task is to assess the risk mediation poses for her client by balancing the client's strengths and weaknesses against those of the other spouse. Once a lawyer determines that a client...presents a high-risk profile, the lawyer generally should try to avoid mediation. Avoidance seems especially important when the client has experienced physical or emotional abuse in the marriage...Some high-risk clients, however, eventually can recover sufficient strength to negotiate effectively with their spouses. For instance, a husband's depression caused by his anticipated loss of a close relationship with his children can subside, and a housewife's low self-esteem and status may increase when she obtains a prestigious new job. Yet recovery usually occurs slowly. Because mediation generally is recommended early in the divorce process, most clients do not have sufficient time to mend.

A different way of finding out how lawyers feel about mediation is to consider the risks that solicitors perceive in their involvement in mediation cases. Bryan (1994, pp.210–15) describes four circumstances that may encourage solicitors to compromise their professionalism. First, the widely held belief that mediation is preferable, because of its informality and potential for retaining family relationships, may mean that lawyers are deterred or distracted from sticking to their tasks of 'formal discovery and the vindication of legal rights' – in other words, a lawyer may be reluctant to ask for hard evidence and/or to assert their client's legal rights for fear of antagonising the other parent; alternatively, the lawyer may simply not attend to such matters once the preoccupying concerns and priorities of mediation take centre stage. Second, Bryan points out that, because mediation has come to be seen as a quicker, cheaper and, overall, more efficient means of resolving disputes between divorcing couples than litigation, lawyers may feel under considerable pressure to help and encourage their client to reach a settlement as speedily as possible. In such circumstances, the solicitor's traditional concerns may, again, lose some of their intensity. The author also acknowledges that lawyers, who frequently carry high workloads, may have their own reasons for 'cutting corners'. Third, Bryan opines that mediators may often insist on the maintenance of an informal atmosphere because of their emphasis on preserving family relationships and, relatedly, because of their belief that displays of open hostility are always unfortunate and to be avoided at all costs. Here, the author's conceptual frame is perhaps at its weakest: the distinction between this (third) and the first category looks less convincing – the solicitor's response to 'pressure' from the mediator will depend, *inter alia*, upon her or his beliefs about the relative efficacy of mediation. Bryan herself (p.213) makes the link as follows:

> Mediation rhetoric feeds on a collective sense of professional guilt, reminding lawyers of what they have heard elsewhere: bad lawyers talk rights, protect legal interests to the detriment of relationship interests, and unnecessarily cause hostility between divorcing parties.

Finally, the author discusses a number of ways in which the lawyer's professional accountability may be diminished. Because, for example, mediation places the onus on parents to come up with an agreement, then the lawyer may feel less responsible if things go wrong.

In continuing the search for how solicitors may perceive mediation, it is helpful to consider the differences between negotiations managed by lawyers and the processes of mediation. Parkinson (1997, pp.19-20) offers the following seven point analysis:

(1) In mediation, both parties are present at meetings and are jointly involved in seeking a settlement – in contrast, lawyers may advise their clients not to talk directly with each other;

(2) Mediation helps parents to keep their children's needs and feelings in the forefront of discussions – negotiations led by solicitors may not do this, giving attention to property and financial matters;

(3) Mediation recognises the links that couples often see between different issues in practical and emotional terms – lawyers, however, are obliged to maintain a separation between arrangements for children and financial issues;

(4) Mediation helps couples design plans to suit their own individual circumstances, whereas lawyers are more likely to go for more traditional arrangements – mediators are seen here as being more likely to encourage parents to design their own settlements;

(5) Arrangements worked out between the parties themselves are more likely to last – whereas deals struck by lawyers, or court orders, are less likely to secure the parents' commitment;

(6) Mediation has a number of objectives: settlement is not the only one – lawyers, in contrast, may take a shorter term view with achieving an agreement seen as the key objective;

(7) Mediation involves face-to-face discussions between those directly involved while solicitors employ the, often circuitous and time consuming, exchange of documents and letters.

In their respective divorce practices, mediators and lawyers thus adopt different priorities and employ different, albeit frequently overlapping, discourses. Mediators push for the preservation of relationship and attempt to be even-handed in their dealings with the two parties, while lawyers seek to protect their own client's interests. Solicitors offer legal advice to their clients while mediators provide information. There is clearly a need for both approaches and languages in the context of divorce and separation but it is also difficult to imagine an entirely peaceful co-existence for mediators and solicitors. Bryan (p.215) concludes that:

> ....a lawyer always should complete formal discovery before mediation, and should insist that the agreement reflect the substantive legal rights of her client. In so doing, she must expect and be prepared to ignore mediator disapproval and hostility

perhaps leading to the contention that lawyers not only enhance conflict between divorcing parents but may also antagonise mediators, albeit in the legitimate pursuance of their professional obligations.

Returning to the question of how solicitors perceive mediation, it is useful to distinguish between child-focused and all-issues, or comprehensive, mediation because, of course, opinions may vary markedly on these two types of intervention. As identified earlier in this section, all-issues mediation has come to be widely regarded as superior to the child-focused form, in terms of its effectiveness in achieving meaningful settlements. But might this level of esteem also be felt by solicitors? There are some indications from the literature that this may not be the case: Walker *et al.* (1994), for example, carried out a small-scale survey of solicitors (n=21) who had all worked with parents who had experience of all-issues mediation. The researchers found that solicitors were more likely to regard children's issues, rather than property and finance matters, as being suitable for mediation. Nevertheless, they also concluded that, overall, it was still possible to offer the following set of categories (p.149) by which solicitors might be divided on their attitudes towards mediation:

(1) The 'enthusiasts', who were knowledgeable about mediation and committed to its development;
(2) The 'sympathetic', who were willing to use mediation but selective and cautious about its further development;
(3) The 'ignorant', who were, as the category unequivocally suggests, somewhat separate from an informed position and discourse;

(4) The 'hostile', although the authors provide less evidence for the validity of this category.

The value of this framework must remain in some doubt, given both the size of the sample and the means by which the 21 interviewees were chosen – some of the solicitors, for example, had actually been trained by the Family Mediators Association and it is reasonable to believe that they would have been much more likely to be both enthusiastic and informed about mediation. Nevertheless, the categories do look to be in line with common-sense expectations and might usefully be tested in further, larger scale studies.

## Judges, Courts and Mediation

> I was faced with a choice of either going to mediation or having a judge high-handedly deciding what is best for my kids. What would you choose?

The fact that judges are able to be prescriptive in regard to contact and residence arrangements for children is likely to act as a significant 'incentive' for parents to reach agreement during mediation. Having this 'final word' is undoubtedly a key aspect of the judge's role but there are a number of other dimensions worthy of consideration. Although participants in the Essex study had not been asked to give their views on the role of the district judge in their case, a range of illuminating references were made to this important aspect of county court mediation. The points raised are understandably diverse and are not presented as representative of wider constituencies, although an attempt has been made to locate them in more general conceptual categories.

First, there are a set of comments that call for judges to take a more active mode of involvement: to do more or to do things differently. The following example makes a request for the judge to emphasise the need to keep to the mediation agreement:

> I asked for the children to be supervised but this was not stuck to. The judge could have stressed the importance of the guidelines, as I feel my ex-partner does not think of what he says in front of the children,

and it is interesting that this mother also expressed a wish for a more assertive approach to have been taken by both mediator and solicitor. She reported that the mediation settlement had failed to stand the test of time because of her ex-partner's behaviour, and suggests that, had court personnel been more emphatic about the importance of keeping to the agreed arrangements, then the outcome might have been significantly improved. There was a need for further reinforcement, for an enhanced expression of the solemnity of the occasion and of the settlement achieved. Other suggestions were for judges to be able to meet the child or children concerned:

> If my son was happy with the arrangement before mediation, should he have been asked his view? As he is 10 years old, I think the Judge could speak to a child...

> The boys wanted to speak to the Judge to give their view – The boys – especially the eldest had suffered verbal abuse and had seen me suffer...

while one father had evidently gone to court hoping for an immediate hearing before the judge:

> I was not expecting that type of hearing, I had trouble in seeing my daughter and I was expecting a court hearing where a judge would be when I went in the mediation room,

an expectation that may be even more remarkable given that the man had been legally represented and accompanied by his solicitor on the day.

A considerable number of Essex study parents had not been convinced about the value of mediation in their, respective, case and said that they would have preferred to have had matters heard and decided upon directly by a district judge. The following illustrative example may be construed as a call for a more rigorous environment, of evidence and the formal establishment of facts – in other words, for the sort of legalistic, 'adversarial' meeting that mediation can be seen to have displaced:

> I think it would be much fairer for a case to be put before a judge and for him to make a decision on the best interests of the children concerned. My ex-wife was able to make up a complete tissue of lies and basically get away with what she had done (i.e. abducted my children) and walk away with everything she wanted. I have ended up with a more or less worthless agreement and no court order and am completely dissatisfied with the whole system. I think it is appalling and will result in the relationship with my children being damaged.

Relatedly, there were accounts of having returned to court, or of waiting to do so, after mediation settlements had broken down:

> ...I am having to go back to court because my ex-husband has not kept any of the promises he made to me, to his solicitor and my solicitor and to the mediator...this is going to be more expensive and the children keep asking why nothing is happening after I had told them that their father and I had sorted things out...what was the point of it in the first place? With hindsight it would have been much better just to let my solicitor and the judge handle it, which is what I hope will happen as soon as we get a date fixed.

Second, in contrast, there are commentaries which favourably compare mediation with its more traditional alternative:

> I am not a confident person but feel I was able to present my case better than if I went in front of a Judge. Obviously as a legal aid case I am able to put more feeling and understanding forward than a solicitor might,

and it is possible to say that the relative 'informality' of mediation is highly regarded by many people – who feel more able to speak freely and, as a result, to express themselves 'as a parent'. The opportunity opened by mediation for parents to present their views with emotion looks to be one of its main advantages. Similarly, mediation may allow parents who feel especially vulnerable the chance to catch their breath, steady themselves and take an active part in negotiations. On the other hand, it would not be fair to conclude that all parents experience mediation as 'informal': some clearly find its customs and conventions oppressive and call for a more relaxed approach by mediators, an important insight that is considered further in chapter 6.

Finally, the Essex study data includes a small number of replies that, arguably, demonstrate a less than wholesome approach adopted by the mediator:

> Basically the mediator told me I should agree because if I didn't then the Judge would do it for me. He said it like a threat in a way and this can be very hard for you if you don't have anyone on your side like a solicitor to back you up.

Given the pressure on mediators to facilitate settlements, to achieve a standard success rate and to process a set number of meetings in a short time-span, it is easy to believe that perhaps a few will resort to employing such 'threats'. Practitioners and their managers may no doubt wish to consider how to guard against such unprofessional practice. If intentional, such conduct is unwise; if inadvertent, it suggests poor communication skills. However, there is a need for caution here as perceptions and meanings construed may be shaped to a considerable extent by the tensions of the mediation event and, after all, the difference between the provision of factual information – 'if you are unable to agree then the Judge may take a decision' – and coercion, on the part of the mediator, may be little more than inflective.

There are two further characteristics of county court mediation that require consideration in this context. First, county courts and their ancillary personnel may themselves produce a certain ambience, which some people will find threatening. Deeper associations with criminal courts may also cause anxiety and shape expectations, while necessary security measures can help generate tension. Second, despite their frequent visits to court premises and familiarity with protocols and routines, family court officers are obliged to ply their trade 'away from home' and this may have a number of consequences, depending on local circumstances. On the basis of observational visits made to county courts, it is possible to suggest that mediators may experience some measure of tension because they have to rely upon and fit in with a number of 'other' agendas. For example, there may be stiff competition for accommodation, with lawyers seeking private space for advising their clients – county courts can, at times, be very busy places. Relatedly, mediators are called upon to undertake a certain number of sessions within a given time, in part so as to comply with the judge's agenda and availability. This is not to infer that the experienced family court officer is unable to manage these additional pressures, the intention is rather to point them out as potentially significant aspects of a rounded account of professional practice in this area. Of course, it is possible to imagine more taxing difficulties: mediation meetings, for example, may occasionally not proceed quite as smoothly nor as speedily as expected and, should, by chance, the day's programme contain a number of such sessions, then mediators may experience a considerable discomfort, that may be exacerbated, to some extent at least, by the need to fit in with external demands. Finally, mediators at court may miss the ready access to managers, colleagues and support personnel that working on their own territory would provide. In the most difficult cases, a restricted route to consultation and counsel from experienced colleagues could be particularly worrisome.

## Conclusion

Lawyers evidently make an important contribution to mediation proceedings and it is possible to say that, overall, their presence during meetings is welcomed by parents in dispute. Nevertheless, there are a number of issues that perhaps need to be more closely considered by the professionals involved in mediation, most worthy of note being the case where one parent is legally accompanied during mediation while the other parent is not. Given the accepted wisdom that not to engage a solicitor in divorce proceedings is potentially risky, having one party represented looks to be questionable in the interests of fairness. If mediators are charged with the job of ensuring an even balance of power then the presence of only one solicitor may reasonably be regarded as a prohibitory factor. On the other hand, there may be certain situations where the balance of power is so skewed in favour of one party that the additional support provided by a solicitor may serve to redress the inequality: cases with a history of partner abuse or mental health needs may readily fall into this category. Needless to say the issue is complex but there must be a strong argument in favour of related practice being urgently and systematically reviewed.

Professions characteristically guard what they see as their territory and the fact that lawyers have been and, indeed, continue to be wary of the development of mediation services comes as no real surprise. It is also possible to say that some measure of circumspection is all to the good, acting as an exacting, yet constructive, challenge to mediators to provide an account of what they do, in effect to ensure that the 'excessive claims' (Wilding, 1982), sometimes made by professionals, are subjected to effective scrutiny and duly limited. Many lawyers may be particularly cautious in relation to all-issues mediation for two reasons: first, they may feel especially threatened by its proximity to what they consider to be their own expert domain; and second, they may have a greater affinity to the child-focused mode because its main practitioners are court-based personnel, with whom they may have frequent contact. On the other hand, those solicitors who are well-informed, possibly FMA trained, are likely to take an opposite stance, emphasising instead the limitations of child-focused intervention. The picture is therefore complex, although certainly not beyond comprehension.

The role played by district judges in mediation looks to be significant, at least in an indirect sense, and the immediacy of intervention suggests that, in county court dispute resolution, the role may be especially important. Mediators and solicitors need to be sensitive to the impact on parents and take steps to ensure, as far as is possible, that no undue pressure is placed on reaching a settlement. Agreements made in such circumstances may be of little long-term value, although it is fair to add that a certain amount of 'pressure' – some way short of coercion – may often be appropriate.

The Essex study has provided some support for the notion that mediation undertaken on court premises and involving 'legal' personnel has both advantages and disadvantages in regard to the additional 'formality' engendered. As already mentioned in chapter 2, formality may produce an unhelpful tension while, on the other hand, also grant an appropriate weight, dignity or solemnity to proceedings. In this chapter, the same pair of opposing possibilities has been apparent in the data provided by parents concerning their experiences and opinions of legal representation.

Finally, there is no little irony in the high financial costs incurred by many parents in employing legal representatives: after all, mediation has been championed as a less expensive alternative to litigation – to discover, therefore, that bills running into thousands of pounds are being run up before, alongside and after mediation proceedings may come as something of a surprise to many of its keenest protagonists. Having a detailed written agreement is, of course, no guarantee of future co-operation and may simply provide a further set of opportunities to continue the dispute, with correspondence between respective solicitors unabated, while parents who are unable to achieve a settlement may also incur a series of unpredicted and unwelcome costs.

# 6 The Best and Worst of Mediation

This chapter reviews a number of professional assumptions about 'best practice' in the light of service user testimony. Mediators set boundaries and groundrules within sessions, they are expected to manage opportunities and constraints, and considerable discretion is theirs to employ in the use of methods and modes of intervention. However, the constitution and procedure of county court mediation are also formed and held within wider frames – of law, tradition and policy – hence, the chapter also examines a range of such factors that, in effect, set the scene for the unfolding and artistry of practice.

## Co-mediation

The potential advantages and disadvantages of co-mediation, within one and across disciplines, have been helpfully described by Parkinson (1997, pp.72–78). Key advantages include the additional 'balance' offered, the scope for different points of view, a check on oversight and the support provided for the mediator by the presence and involvement of their colleague. Parkinson identifies a range of possible difficulties including cost, competition and confusion: co-mediators may also 'take sides', becoming split, or 'team up' to dominate one or more of the parents.

As yet there are insufficient data concerning the use of co-mediation to allow any broad quantification, although it is possible to say that there are steep variations in practice across mediation agencies and from one geographical area to another. The study by Morgan (1996) shows that parents in West Glamorgan had been just as likely to have two mediators present as one, while parents attending Essex county courts were much more likely to have one mediator only – 84 per cent of participants said that there had been one mediator. However, within the county of Essex, parents in Southend were much more likely than those in Chelmsford to have two mediators present: such variation would appear to be a result of practitioner preference, rather than policy or different types of cases in the two local areas.

In the Essex study the number of mediators present at the meeting was afforded little significance by parents. Some participants said that one mediator had been sufficient, while a small number felt that two had been or would have been advantageous, most often because of the 'gender-mix' that was or would have been afforded.

Interestingly, parents in West Glamorgan had, overall, been less concerned with this issue: 52 per cent had indicated that, in cases involving two mediators, it would not matter if both mediators were of the same gender.

As described in chapter 4, having more than one mediator was also seen by some women as offering a measure of protection. Nevertheless, it is possible to say that, overall, Essex study parents had not been especially concerned with whether there had been one or more mediator present. Possibly this may be related to the fact that they had played no part in deciding on the number of mediators to be involved but it may also be that the advantages and disadvantages of co-working are mainly for mediators rather than for parents in dispute. In reporting the Newcastle research findings, for example, Walker *et al.* (1994) point out that, while most mediators had extolled the virtues of co-practice, the emphasis had been placed on the benefits for them as practitioners (p.123). In part this might be explained by the (then) novelty of comprehensive mediation – mediators would especially welcome the support of colleagues when delivering a new mode of service – but it is also not unreasonable to argue that parents may be relatively unaware of and/or unconcerned by the sophistications and nuances of co-mediation. In the absence of a clearly stated rationale by mediators, parents may assume that whatever is offered to them must be both normative and relatively unremarkable. Asking them whether they would have preferred one or two mediators to have been present may therefore be less productive than initially predicted.

## Preparation and Expectations

> A little bit more information how the system works, directed at unrepresented persons like myself would take out the 'walking in blind' feeling I had at the start of the meeting.

The professional mediation literature emphasises the need to prepare parents properly before the initial session takes place and, in models incorporating a series of meetings, to use the first session as an opportunity to clarify expectations and groundrules (Haynes, 1993, pp.18–20; Parkinson, 1997, pp.125–159). An understanding of the importance of preparing the 'client' is also apparent in the legal literature, although it is necessary to draw a distinction between two very different senses of the word 'preparation', in this context. First, preparation may simply mean that the client is informed about mediation in a relatively neutral or objective fashion: second, in sharp contrast, 'preparation' can be regarded as a way of coaching the parent for a form of contest or performance within a highly politicised milieu. Bryan (1994), for example, argues that parents need to be alerted to the common pitfalls and difficulties characteristic of family mediation, including the pressure to reach a settlement, the focus on relationship to the exclusion of individual rights and the 'seduction of informality' (p.216). The author also recommends that lawyers should assist their clients in 'self-understanding' so that, if a parent feels guilty about something, she or he may be encouraged to anticipate and resist attempts by the mediator, by the ex-spouse or by the other lawyer to manipulate that guilt.

Findings from the Essex study suggest that many parents feel unprepared for their mediation meeting – 78 per cent of participants said that they had no expectations about mediation based on previous experience or knowledge. Predicting what might happen during mediation was therefore a matter of surmise for many parents and there are examples of both surprise and frustration when the expectations, that parents did bring, and reality failed to concur. It is clear that some parents make extensive preparation for the event, only to be informed on the day that the meeting will not address the data and documents assembled:

> We are seen separately. Then go in together and in my case I had the letter from my solicitor arranging times and the children had wrote to their father. The mediator didn't want to know about any of that. I had kept a diary of all the times he's let them down. I do think that some of that should have been taken into account.

This is not to say that such 'evidence' should be presented, the point is that best practice would aim to prepare parents adequately for their session, which must include making every effort to avoid surprises about what is and is not permissible during mediation. Essex Family Court Service provides parents with an information leaflet some time before mediation takes place and, indeed, invite further enquiries concerning its purpose, priorities and process. Similarly, legal representatives might be expected to play an important preparatory role (chapter 5 has provided an account of the part played by solicitors in mediation). However, the Essex study research suggests that, of those parents who do have expectations of mediation, most are likely to have gained them from their own experience of previous mediation sessions. There were references to one, two or three prior mediation meetings, although a few appear to have been in settings other than county court. Other sources quoted were 'discussions with solicitors' and 'directions hearings', while only one parent mentioned the leaflet provided by EFCS. The value of information leaflets may thus be open to question, although Morgan's study (1996) found that most parents who had received a leaflet described their understanding of the mediation process as 'quite good', rather than 'not very good' or 'very good'. However, there are grounds to suggest that contemporary practice in this aspect of mediation might usefully be reviewed by Family Court Services and CAFCASS. There is certainly still some considerable ground to be made up in helping parents prepare for mediation and, with this in mind, some form of preliminary meeting could be advantageous – Walker *et al.* (1994, p.86) report that mediation users in the Newcastle study said that they had been well informed by the combination of leaflet and introductory interview. There is little sense in the Essex study data of 'coaching' by legal representatives, in the way advocated by Bryan (1994), although the following words show that some parents do indeed receive a measure of tactical preparation for their session:

> In the weeks running up to mediation I met my solicitor on two occasions, with my new 'friend' also there, so to prepare myself for going to mediation at court. Some of the time was spent with my solicitor telling us what to expect from the mediator and things I should avoid saying, like no dragging up the past or saying what a total waste of space my ex- has been, not paying maintenance and that, but also to think about what to do if things start to go against me.

Mediators also need to be, and to feel, prepared for their endeavours with parents in dispute and, in particular, they should have access to significant information about the two parties and in regard to the child or children concerned. Such parental information would include any history and risk of violence, race and ethnic origin, the need for special facilities for disabled people, etceteras. For children, such data would embrace the existence and details of any special needs and information about past or present social work involvement. The Essex study suggests that almost one in ten of the families included at least one child with a current social worker, although only one in a hundred families had at least one child on the Child Protection Register. The reasons for social work involvement included educational, behavioural and health-related factors in addition to cases of poor parenting and child protection.

As mentioned in chapter 2, user expectations of public services are frequently low and this is apparent from analysis of the Essex study responses. However, most participants had no prior expectations of mediation and, of those that did have expectations, most had derived them from their own previous experience of mediation. A need for caution in interpreting the finding is therefore raised – after all, many participants will have been obliged to return to mediation because previous settlements had broken down, meaning that they would be more likely to hold low expectations.

Asking Essex study users whether they thought that mediation, in principle, was a 'good thing' also produced data pertinent to the issue of expectations – in the sense that the enquiry encourages the making of a distinction by the participant between the ideal and the reality of mediation. Eighty-four per cent of Essex study parents felt that, in principle, mediation was, indeed, a good thing and there were three major themes apparent in their replies: first, the opportunity to discuss matters in the presence of an unbiased, third party; second, a means of finding a compromise when parents have different starting points or have reached an impasse – in many cases, the mediator is here seen as being able to offer a way forward or new insight that breaks the deadlock; and, third, as a less stressful 'diversion' from court. There follows a set of illustrative quotations from Essex study parents:

> In theory it should be a good thing because two people who are at loggerheads have to sit down sometime and they will then want someone who is fair to help them talk to each other;

> It allows an outside party to bring to light issues that might not have previously been given much thought and to work out better arrangements for the sake of the children involved;

> If it can keep people out of court which is most anxiety provoking then it must be a good thing to try to do. I was terrified at thinking about going to court which I have never done in my life before.

Of those parents who replied that mediation, in principle, was not a good thing, the most common explanation was that it needed to have more weight, or authority, so that agreed arrangements could be made to 'stick'. Other accounts made reference to the high financial cost of mediation and to the shortcomings of not including the child's viewpoint. However, many responses suggested that the participant had experienced no little difficulty in maintaining the distinction between ideal and reality promoted by the survey item.

## Mediators as Parents and People

In order to gain and retain the confidence of parents, mediators need a great deal of knowledge and an array of skills. Much of this expertise comes from a familiarity with, and an understanding of, family court procedures, coupled with assets acquired through professional training. However, successful mediation practice also appears to call for, at least in the eyes of some parents, a set of additional qualities. First, there is need for a capacity to connect with other people that draws from personal maturity or 'worldliness':

> The mediators should be more people orientated and approachable. I do not appreciate being offered advice from someone who obviously has no grasp of the real issues or how these affect relationships,

and, second, an understanding and empathy derived from similar experiences of loss and suffering:

> A person to conduct the proceedings who has experienced the break up of their relationship, however long, who has experienced the pain and suffering that I am feeling to be denied a natural relationship between father and son.

It would be wholly unreasonable to hold such specific expectations of mediators but, on the other hand, practitioners should be sensitive to the feelings that parents may experience. A profound sense of loss, anger, isolation and being overwhelmed are just some of the emotions commonplace in this context and many parents would argue that mediators require a considerable level of maturity, in addition to professional skills, in order to practise effectively in this area.

In the literature, the question of what makes one mediator more proficient than another tends to be answered in terms of expert knowledge, experience (as a mediator), having a pro-active approach and providing a sense of structure, purpose and control (Parkinson, 1997, pp.346–348). The Essex study findings thus offer an opportunity to review such traditional assumptions and it is reasonable to contend that some parents may attribute a higher level of expertise to a mediator who is able to demonstrate an empathy founded upon similar, personal experiences to their own.

Overall, mediator effectiveness may therefore be most wisely conceptualised as flowing from a complex interaction between different sets of variables – these would include mediator and service user characteristics, the nature and circumstances of the dispute, and factors concerned with the dynamics of the couple's inter-relationship.

Of course, the notion of 'mediators as people' summons attention to a range of social, as well as personal, issues. Race, ethnicity, gender, socio-economic class and sexual orientation are constructs that not only describe significant ways in which people differ from each other but also point to potential affiliations, oppressions and conflicts of interest. Questions of 'empathy' and 'gaining the confidence' of service users thus come to have a much broader meaning than a locus around professional expertise could allow.

Walker *et al.* (1994) conclude that the responses they received from mediators:

> ...would suggest that the ideal comprehensive mediation case would involve two well-educated, middle-class people, both in employment, jointly owning a house... (p.122).

Given the apparent lack of attention paid by the Newcastle study researchers to the race and ethnicity of mediation users, it is tempting to suggest that the ideal case would also involve two white, English parents. However, it is important to acknowledge the fact that mediation research in the UK has generally ignored these issues (Parkinson, 1997, p.327), in effect producing a mirror image of professional preoccupation and omission. A similar state of affairs presides in the USA, where Taylor and Sanchez (1991) have called for practice to be adapted to meet the needs of Hispanic and other minority groups. The Essex study may also be challenged, on the grounds that it fails to concern itself with the race and ethnicity of parents undergoing county court mediation. The fact that no pertinent data are collected by Essex Family Court Service simply reinforces the need for researchers to address the issue: an account of the study's limitations, in this and other domains, is provided in the appendices.

The absence of basic information about the use made of mediation services by black parents in dispute may be understood as one facet of institutional, or organisational, racism (Dominelli, 1997, pp.129–147). Family court services need to possess such data in order to plan and monitor their work with black families and one way of encouraging them to collect the information would have been to include a section within the *Family Law Act 1996* obliging them to do so – as an example, section 95(1)(b) of the *Criminal Justice Act 1991* calls upon the Secretary of State to produce annual reports of information for the purpose of

> ...facilitating the performance by such persons of their duty to avoid discriminating against any persons on the ground of race or sex or any other improper ground,

and the arrival and implementation of this requirement have ensured that all area probation services have assembled appropriate data on the ethnicity and race of the offenders they work with. It is difficult to envisage why a similar spur to improvement has not been provided in the mediation field. As things stand, family court services are simply unable to rebut suspicions or allegations of institutional racism because they cannot supply anything more than anecdotal evidence. They are required by national standards (Home Office, 1994) to ensure that their work is free from improper discrimination on any ground, including race, gender, sexual orientation, age, disability, religion, literacy and language ability (para. 1.13) but, without even the most rudimentary data being available, it is difficult to see how such laudable ambitions might be met. In the absence of clear policy, founded on accurate information, the development of practice in this area proceeds much more slowly and haphazardly than it needs to: questions of how mediators can best hone their skills in relation to work with members of ethnic minority groups remain at the margins of organisational and professional interest. Finally, similar arguments might be constructed around other areas of difference and, of the categories listed by National Standards above, 'literacy' appears to have received very little attention to date.

## Setting and Policing the Groundrules for Effective Communication

> Both parties knew what was to be discussed at the meeting. The setting of parameters made it easier to focus my thoughts and forget the hurt.

The need for mediators to set 'groundrules' – in effect, to encourage certain behaviours and to prohibit others – alongside an announcement of the main purposes of mediation is clearly recognised in the literature. However, because of the temporal limitations of county court mediation, practitioners face significant problems in ensuring that parents adequately grasp such rules of engagement. Furthermore, mediation meetings are frequently tense affairs, especially at their inception, and it is possible that many parents may fail to understand fully what is being relayed in the mediator's opening address. On the other hand, the Essex study data provides plenty of evidence that mediators perform an important role in 'policing' behaviour and in ensuring a sense of fair play:

> The best thing was that the mediator was there to keep a check on tempers and to make sure that nobody could just have their way all the time...she was very fair about that without making one feel she was on their side or against what they said.

Mediators are also expected to provide a 'buffer' between ex-spouses and, in part, this can be achieved through the setting and policing of groundrules. Many women feel especially vulnerable in the presence of their ex-partner and it is incumbent upon mediators both to recognise this aspect of mediation and to ensure that a sense of orderliness, with clear parameters of acceptable behaviour, is quickly established and maintained throughout the session. One mother describes it thus:

> It took control of a situation I had no control over anymore. I didn't want to be in contact with my ex-husband but the children still needed him.

Sixty-eight per cent of parents who participated in the Essex study reported that groundrules had been set by the mediator and, of these, 88 per cent had felt that the rules had been applied effectively. The fact that almost one third of participants, who responded to the questionnaire item, said that groundrules had not been stipulated may be regarded as less than satisfactory, although it is possible that some parents may have simply failed to remember, while others may have formed their reply on the basis of how effectively the rules had been applied during the session, rather than whether or not they had been announced at its commencement.

Of those participants who felt that groundrules had been applied effectively, most described the emphasis placed by the mediator on a need to 'keep to the point' of the meeting, rather than moving into issues from the past. Other rules identified were: no interrupting; no arguing; no maligning the other party; keeping to time; and nothing to be written down. The following quotations are presented in order to illustrate these themes:

> If accusations were made about the other party the meeting would stop. Also that the meeting was to be conducted in a civil manner and allow the other person to speak;

> The mediator intervened when my ex-wife strayed from the matter of contact and started to say bad things about my friends and family;

> We were not to bring in why we were divorced and don't get on. We were kept purely on the issue of the child's welfare. It was very good;

> Basically, no interrupting and no arguing. He butted in. When I walked out of the room the rules were re-iterated. My solicitor got me back in the room.

Of those participants who felt that groundrules, though set, had not been applied properly, the main reasons given were: the 'other party' had been insufficiently checked from interrupting, being unpleasant or threatening; unsatisfactory time-keeping; not keeping to the point of the session; and one party feeling that the mediator had been more likely to listen to the other parent. There was also a small number of replies that focused on the style adopted by the mediator in their setting and upholding of groundrules: some parents had evidently experienced that style as 'patronising':

> ...we were treated like school kids...an absolute insult, [and]

> It's bad enough having to be coming to court without someone half your age looking down their nose and telling you that you've been a naughty boy by interrupting. My ex-wife told one lie after another and I was supposed to sit there and listen to her rubbish which I could not do.

However, such sentiments were rare and, overall, it is possible to conclude that mediators both prescribe and operate groundrules effectively. It is significant that, when parents were asked to identify one, especially good thing about their experience of mediation, the image of a structured, managed and fair opportunity to establish communication and agreement may readily be drawn from replies.

## Helping Settlements Last and Improving the Process of Mediation

> I would make the terms agreed a legally binding agreement – which would become an offence if the parent with care did not adhere to them.

As already discussed in chapter 2 of this essay, many Essex study parents highlighted the need to have a written copy of the mediation agreement and the need to make the agreement more binding, in their suggestions for how settlements might be encouraged to endure. However, there were also many requests for an opportunity to meet separately with the mediator before the session. There were two main reasons given for such a meeting: first, so as to provide an opportunity to express specific concerns about the other party, a suggestion for improving current practice made particularly by women; and, second, to relay detailed information about the history and contemporary circumstances of the dispute. The call for a separate meeting with the mediator was also made by many participants in the research study by Walker *et al.* (1994, pp.58–59), although the emphasis there was placed on the former of the two reasons given by Essex study parents, with the majority of requests for a preliminary meeting again coming from women. Given the need for a much greater urgency around the issue of violence, the introduction of a brief, prefatory meeting into present mediation practice appears to offer a great deal. Similarly, issues of mental health, disability, ethnicity, race and culture might be more readily recognised and addressed.

The opportunity to meet separately with the mediator beforehand may be conceptualised as a way of improving the process of mediation or as a means of enhancing the outcome(s) of mediation. It is not always clear from the questionnaire data what had been in the participant's mind when making their suggestion. However, a number of proposals were aimed specifically at the processual aspect of mediation. For example, as discussed fully in chapter 4, the availability of separate waiting areas was seen as particularly important, especially by women.

## Overall Satisfaction and Fair Treatment

Parkinson (1997, p.330) helpfully summarises findings on satisfaction rates, indicating that UK, Australian and American user studies show levels of satisfaction within the 60–85 per cent range (Pearson and Thoennes, 1984; Kelly, 1989; Irving and Benjamin, 1992; Bordow and Gibson, 1994). However, there are grounds for caution in making immediate comparisons given the different concerns and methods of the various studies included. For example, the research by Walker *et al.* (1994) employs two distinct measures: satisfaction with the process of mediation; and satisfaction with the outcome of mediation. For the former, the researchers report that approximately two thirds of 'clients' had declared themselves as satisfied with the way mediation had been carried out, with 10 per cent expressing dissatisfaction (p.60). For the latter measure, addressing the outcome of mediation, about one half of comprehensive mediation users had felt satisfied while 18 per cent had been dissatisfied – the comparable figures for child-focused mediation were 38 per cent and 26 per cent respectively. As can be seen from this cursory collation, the authors' reporting of the Newcastle findings raises a number of concerns: first, why are the figures, apparently, incomplete; and, second, why are the satisfaction results, especially for child-focused mediation, so much lower than the normal range suggested by Parkinson? The waters are made even cloudier by a further measure adopted by the Newcastle researchers in the context of a three years follow-up study: participants were asked to say whether they were 'glad they had opted to use mediation' or 'whether they wished they had not gone' (McCarthy and Walker, 1996, p.8). The results reported are that 63 per cent of respondents were glad they had opted for mediation, 25 per cent wished they had not gone and the remainder had no feelings either way. Again there was a sharp difference between the two modes with 82 per cent of users of comprehensive mediation and 54 per cent of users of child-focused mediation expressing a positive appraisal. Although there is some comfort to be drawn from the relative completeness of these later figures, the apparent conflation of outcome and process, following their earlier distinction, arguably stands on rather shaky ground.

In the Essex study, 70 per cent of participants had felt that their mediation session had been of an acceptable, or better, standard, while 30 per cent had been dissatisfied or very dissatisfied. As already mentioned in chapter 2, there was a close association between the level of satisfaction expressed and whether or not the mediation settlement had still been in place when the satisfaction question was put. However, it is likely that some participants had not made the distinction between the process and the outcome of the mediation meeting, despite the aim and wording of the questionnaire item. A number of other variables were also found to be closely associated with 'satisfaction': the duration of the settlement; whether or not the presence of solicitors had been perceived as helpful; whether or not groundrules had been applied effectively; whether or not the participant had felt able to say everything they wanted to; whether or not mediation had, in principle, been seen as a 'good thing'; and whether or not the participant had felt unfairly treated. There were significant, but less strong associations with: whether or not the participant had felt that something else could have been done at mediation to help secure arrangements; whether or not mediation had been helpful in coming to new arrangements after the initial ones had changed; for women only, whether or not the participant had been legally represented; whether or not the participant had felt that the presence of solicitors, in principle, was a good thing; whether or not the participant had been concerned at siting opposite the other party during mediation; and, again for women only, whether or not the two parties had sat opposite one another during mediation.

It is clear that county court practitioners in Essex are regarded highly by parents in terms of their delivery of 'equal opportunities'. Eighty-four per cent of participants said that they had been treated fairly in regard to issues of gender, race, age, religion, etceteras and, of the 16 per cent who had felt unfairly treated, there were no references to race, age, sexual orientation, only one example of a religious bias and two references to socio-economic class:

> I was judged. I was discriminated against because I was unemployed. In fact, I felt I was treated as a second-class citizen which indeed I was.

Gender, however, was a common theme. As already discussed in chapter 3, for male participants, there was a sense of having been discriminated against because of social assumptions about the relative importance of fathers and mothers to their children. In contrast, for women, the sense of unfairness related to the 'burden of care' and to a lack of sensitivity to the issue of domestic violence, already discussed in chapter 4.

Finally, there are a set of replies that portray a one-sidedness on the part of the mediator(s), not explicitly related to gender or other 'difference', for example:

> When I was in the mediation on my own there seemed to be a biased attitude towards the other side, by trying to pressure me into an answer and immediate decision.

This more general aspect of 'fair treatment' was also addressed by asking parents whether or not they had 'felt able to say everything they really wanted to the mediator(s)' and, here, expressions of dissatisfaction were more frequently made. Of the 29 per cent of participants who had not felt able to say everything they wanted to: most had felt that the mediator had been biased towards the other party; many said that they had not been allowed to bring important (to them) information to the mediator's attention – being made to feel that such material was irrelevant or trivial; others had been unsettled by the event or location, for example:

> I felt completely overwhelmed by being dragged to court so hence I couldn't remember things – forgetting sentences when I started them etc.,

> [or, being interrupted by the other party]

> I wasn't given an equal amount of time, every time I tried to talk my ex-wife would shout and scream to get her own opinion across,

and, again, some women had been intimidated by their ex-partner. There were also many references to the pressures of limited time and to feeling that an agreement 'had' to be reached:

> Felt as if the mediator was in a hurry and didn't want to listen to what appeared to her as trivial matters [and]

> I felt all they wanted was a quick agreement and they were not interested in what the children felt or wanted.

A small number of participants identified 'procedural rules' as the source of difficulty, for example:

> Because he applied for residence/custody he was allowed to speak first. He did a long speech with a lot of lies so I had to remember them all and

correct him on all issues when it was my turn to talk. After that I didn't get a chance to say anything else,

raising intriguing questions around ordering, groundrules and, in particular, the stipulation against note-taking during mediation.

Given that one county court mediation session is all that is received by most parents who reach an agreement, it is hardly surprising that a considerable number will come away feeling that they would have liked to have said more to the mediator(s), while some are likely to feel particularly frustrated by the parameters of their meeting. Against this backcloth, the finding that about seven out of every ten Essex study parents had felt that they had been able to say everything they wanted appears to be worthy of commendation.

## Consulting the Child

It really highlighted that the child's needs must be first, and however much the parents think about each other this must not be allowed to affect the children.

The direct involvement of children in mediation is a relatively recent phenomenon even though conciliation, the forerunner of mediation, had been exclusively concerned with issues of 'custody' and 'access', in which children hold an obvious and important stake. The subsequent expansion of mediation, to encompass matters of property and finance with which children have less apparent interest, has, perhaps paradoxically, accompanied a broad shift towards the inclusion of children. The *Children Act 1989* promoted the idea of ascertaining the wishes and feelings of the child (section 1, the 'welfare checklist') and this was given further momentum by s.11 of the *Family Law Act 1996*. However, it had been recognised in the preceding White Paper that mediators did not act 'for the child', although they were required to 'remind' parents of their responsibilities towards their children (Lord Chancellor's Department, 1995, s.5.32), and a number of commentators have been fiercely critical of: (1) the assumption that securing a parental settlement will automatically be in the best interests of the child; and (2) the absence of independent representation for the child within the mediation process (Freeman, 1996, xiii). The White Paper also acknowledged the rapid shift in thinking about the involvement of children in mediation and predicted that:

...within the not too distant future mediators will be specifically trained to deal appropriately with the interests of children during mediation, and will receive guidance on when and in what circumstances it is appropriate to involve children in mediation (s.5.33).

The representation of children in family proceedings has been a key issue in government consultations leading to the creation of CAFCASS (see chapter 4, Department of Health *et al.* (1998)) and one of the advantages of the new service would appear to be the prospect of a closer integration of welfare and legal representation. Section 64 of the *Family Law Act 1996* allows the Lord Chancellor to devise regulations providing for the separate representation of children, although implementation of this power has been delayed.

There is widespread agreement that full representation is unlikely to be required in most private law cases, although there is also an acceptance that, in cases where a child of sufficient maturity has views that oppose those held by their parents, separate legal advocacy may be appropriate.

Professional opinion is divided on the question of involving children in mediation. Dowling and Gorrell-Barnes (2000), for example, suggest that this may lead to complexities that distract from the key purpose of mediation (pp.186–187) while, on the other hand, Robinson (1999) is able to conclude that the involvement of children in mediation can, overall, be regarded as beneficial (p.140). Different stances are also taken on the issue of timing, with some mediation services involving children only after a settlement has been reached and others including children much earlier in the process (Robinson, 1999, p.141). Haynes (1993) describes his own practice as a mediator of reviewing the settlement with the children, in part to share information but, also, so as to allow children an opportunity to amend the agreement (pp.85–86) and it is interesting to note that the author makes no mention of the earlier involvement of children. This is both a reflection of how swiftly the debate has changed and also a helpful reminder of how deeply embedded professional assumptions can be.

The pertinence of the child's age to the questions of whether and how to include children in mediation has been recognised in the literature: Robinson (1999), for example, provides an account of children's understandings of parental disputes according to their age – two to four year olds are described as often assuming responsibility for having caused their parents to separate, while nine to thirteen year olds may establish alliances with one parent (pp.134–135). However, such helpful ideas need to be viewed alongside the dearth of information available on the children who are actually affected by mediation. Attempting to locate such data, concerned with age, numbers of children in the disordered family, 'other' siblings, half- and step-siblings (that is, children of the family for whom there is no 'dispute'), special needs and whether or not the child is known to a Social Services Department, perhaps on a child protection register, is far from easy. Hence, the following paragraphs are dedicated to providing key data on the children who could be involved in future mediation procedures and to a consideration of how a number of such 'characteristics' might be accommodated.

In the Essex study, information on 754 children was available from family court service records and 448 disordered families were included in the sample. Of these families, 50 per cent had one (study) child only, while 36 per cent had two, and 15 per cent had three or more children. This immediately raises important questions about the involvement of children in mediation, in terms of resourcing, management and representation. First, the fact that some 50 per cent of cases would include more than one child highlights the likelihood that considerable effort might be required on the part of mediators. Second, if children were to be directly included in mediation meetings then the effect upon 'group dynamics' could be profound. Finally, would it be reasonable to assume that, in cases where two or more children are involved, their 'representation', as called for by Freeman earlier in this chapter, might ever be a simple matter? In other words, within a disordered family, is it possible to assume that all the children have the same interests to 'represent'? Clearly, this might not always be the case and it could then be necessary to employ two or more 'representatives' for one family, a potentially expensive and complex procedure.

Of the 754 children, there were 448 sole or eldest, 226 second children, 65 third, 13 fourth and two fifth eldest children. Of the sole or eldest children, 2 per cent were aged less than a year, 24 per cent were aged one, two or three, 21 per cent four, five or six, 28 per cent were aged seven, eight or nine, 17 per cent ten, eleven or twelve, 8 per cent were aged thirteen, fourteen or fifteen, and less than 1 per cent had reached the age of sixteen. Of the 226 cases where there were two or more children, 22 per cent were aged one, two or three, 34 per cent four, five or six, 29 per cent seven, eight or nine, 11 per cent were aged ten, eleven or twelve and 2 per cent were aged thirteen, fourteen or fifteen years. It is easy to see from this, albeit incomplete and simple, analysis that the 'involvement' of children in mediation would require work with: (1) sole children of varying ages; and (2) dyads, triads and larger groups of various ages, for families having more than one child. It is sufficient to say that both areas of practice could be highly demanding in terms of knowledge, skills and costs.

While the general assumption that mediation meetings may proceed without hearing the 'voice' of the child is a contentious one, for older children the case for involvement must surely be all the more difficult to resist. Of course, the definition of 'older' is itself open to debate but it would seem reasonable to set the lower limit at around ten years, by which time children have entered the stage of 'late latency' when

> Loyalty conflicts typically cannot be maintained, probably because they are too painful, and so children often make alignments with one or other parent...a significant proportion of children make strong alliances, and sometimes overtly reject or refuse to visit the other parent (Robinson, 1999, p.135).

In other words, children begin to 'vote with their feet' by the time they reach this developmental phase and the need to take their views into consideration takes on a new urgency. A further ground for choosing 'ten' is that, in the UK, this is the current 'age of criminal responsibility' – the argument being that, if a child is old enough to be charged with a criminal offence, then she or he might also expect to be consulted in the context of mediation. The Essex study findings show that approximately one in five children concerned with county court mediation were aged ten years or above, while 6 per cent were teenagers, again suggesting that significant levels of resource would need to be made available should the policy of including older children in mediation be systematically pursued.

In attempting to predict the demands to be met from the involvement of children in mediation, the question of 'special needs' also looks to be important. In the Essex study, the documentary evidence to hand suggests that 13 per cent of disordered families had at least one child with a special need: most of these children had special educational needs, while others had physical or sensory disabilities or behavioural problems, and a small number suffered from a range of chronic illnesses. There were very few explicit references to mental health needs, although contacts with psychotherapists or psychiatrists are sometimes mentioned in relation to 'behavioural difficulties'. A small number of families included more than one child with a special need.

Given the current emphasis on inter-agency practice, mediators do need to be aware if children have been or are in contact with social services departments and other similar bodies. With the prospect of involving children in mediation, this need would be considerably sharpened, especially in cases where child abuse may have taken place or be suspected. The Essex study figures show that some 14 per cent of families had at least one child 'known to' social services and 9 per cent had at least one child with an allocated social worker, while only 1 per cent of cases included a child on the child protection register. These statistics suggest that mediators might need to consult with social workers in as many as one in seven of their cases, a finding that, again, prompts and informs key questions of resourcing and management. National standards for mediation (Home Office, 1994) make no specific reference to liaison with social services, although paragraph 3.9 indicates that an exception could be made to the normal rule of confidentiality if information came to light concerning a risk of 'serious harm'. Thus, it is possible to commend some amendment to national standards, so as to highlight the need for mediators to be aware of social services involvement, particularly when children have been placed on the child protection register. Furthermore, if mediation practice did begin to include children, then the importance of some preliminary contact between mediator and social worker would be significantly increased.

Finally, in this review of the Essex study data, it is important to acknowledge the interests and views of 'other children', that is siblings, half-siblings and step siblings of the child or children with whom mediation is directly concerned. Sometimes there are older siblings who, effectively, make their own decisions about where they reside and whether or not they have contact with an absent parent. Also, many parents form new partnerships after their divorce or separation that bring, through procreation or inheritance, children who have a stake in mediation arrangements, even though they are not the main subjects of residence or contact disputes. 'Involving the children in mediation' takes on a very different meaning once this factor is properly recognised. The Essex study data suggests that there are 'other children' in perhaps one third of mediation cases, although only a proportion of these children reside with the child or children directly concerned in the mediation process. Unfortunately, the reliability of the data on this final point does not allow a confident quantification – the best than can be said is that, of the 448 Essex study cases, the documentary evidence available shows that 73 had at least one other child living with their mother, 32 with their father and 39 living elsewhere – and, therefore, the findings must be mainly regarded as an invitation and guide for further research.

Lindstein and Meteyard (1996, pp.174–177) argue that the significance of mediation for children can be related to the number of sessions attended by parents: for single meetings, the authors suggest that there are no known effects for children, while the most important repercussions are associated with medium and long term work. By this logic, county court mediation would, therefore, not be expected to have significant outcomes for children, although it is difficult to see how the attainment and persistence of a settlement between parents could fail to have implications for the child or children concerned. This is not to say that the parents' and children's interests are the same, the argument is simply that repercussions for both stakeholders look to be unavoidable. Lindstein and Meteyard also contend that mediators should avoid focusing on the child's needs early on in the mediation process on the grounds that this is likely to bring matters to a halt, essentially because of the couple's 'incomplete separation'.

While county court mediation continues to operate primarily on a 'single session' basis it is difficult to foresee any significant shift towards the direct inclusion of children in proceedings. Rather, it is likely that the use of 'indirect consultation' (Robinson, 1999, p.136) will continue to hold sway and, as a consequence, it is fair to predict that concerns about the representation of the child's interests and wishes will also continue to be expressed in both academic and professional circles. At this point it is necessary to recall from the opening chapter that little is known about the range of practices employed by family court services across the country. In particular, insufficient information is available on the use of a series of meetings leading to an opportunity to reach a settlement, rather than one single session at which the search for an agreement is either achieved or, at least temporarily, abandoned. On the basis of anecdotal evidence, it is possible to conclude that some services do employ more than one meeting but the present wisdom does not allow any justifiable statement about the prevalence of such practice. The use of 'review' meetings designed to allow parents an opportunity to return to the mediating table and discuss how the agreed arrangements are working presents an additional complication for researchers in this area: for example, although the study by Morgan (1996) found that 42 per cent of parents reported having had more than one meeting with the mediator, the status and purpose of the 'further' meetings are left unclear.

## Conclusion

Parents need to feel adequately prepared for mediation and there are grounds to suggest that many do not have a sufficiently clear picture of what to expect. This finding may usefully be placed within the wider context of information provision before and during divorce proceedings. The *Family Law Act 1996* sets in place the need and facility for parties considering divorce to attend an 'information meeting' and considerable debate presently ensues around the question of providing information at this early stage (McCarthy, 2000): various modes of provision have been piloted including one-to-one meetings, computer assisted sessions involving a CD-ROM, group meetings and leaflets sent by post. The Act identifies nine substantive areas which information meetings must cover, including mediation, and it is apparent that only limited attention to each of the areas will be possible. With this in mind, the need for CAFCASS to ensure that parents are prepared for mediation attains a new sense of urgency. The preparation of the mediator is a related matter of considerable significance and the use of an initial meeting could be of enormous value in this context. The early identification of literacy problems, the need for an interpreter, disabilities and of specific anxieties about the 'other party' would no doubt be of great benefit to all concerned.

The lack of attention devoted to the impact of the personal characteristics of the mediator on the process and outcomes of mediation may readily be understood as a concomitant of professionalisation. 'Neutrality' has become the touchstone of good practice, in which detachment and 'objectivity' are presented as positive attributes for mediators to possess and wield in their work with parents in dispute. Expert knowledge and skills come to be regarded as all that is required to practice effectively with a succession of individual 'cases', whoever the persons concerned might be, and whatever groups – by race, religion, extended family, culture or class – those people might have associations with. Within this assumptive world, there is little room for an interest in 'who' the mediator is perceived to be and, of course, the notion of identity can be broadened, so as to encompass aspects of 'community', in addition to those of 'personality'. In other words, questions of who the mediator, and, more generally, of who the mediation service represents come to the fore. This avenue of analysis therefore makes it is possible to trace a difficult tension for mediators to resolve. Put sharply, in question form, how does the commitment to professional detachment square with having an empathy for, and connectedness with, individuals and their communities? Finding a balance between these sets of conflicting demands looks to be no easy task but it is incumbent upon mediators to ensure that their preoccupation with professional neutrality does not begin to feel like indifference or aloofness to those on the receiving end. Similarly, managers have a responsibility to avoid the slide towards an actuarial fixation on 'cases, throughput and outcomes', the hallmark of managerialism. It must be said that, at present, there is some evidence to suggest that an appropriate balance has been struck by practitioners and by their managers: the Essex study findings indicate that county court mediators are to be congratulated, both on their even-handedness and on their delivery of equal opportunities. Alongside the high rating of overall satisfaction expressed by service users, this exhibition of 'fairness' adds to the positive appraisal of mediation practice. However, there is no room for complacency given the changes taking place in society, particularly in regard to its multi-cultural constitution, and it is already likely that, in other areas of the UK, the need to develop family court services is much more pressing than in counties such as Essex. One of the first duties for CAFCASS to undertake must surely be to highlight the urgent need for data regarding the race and ethnicity of mediation users to be collected. Ensuring that feedback is sought from black and Asian parents, on their experience of mediation, also looks to be a priority for the new agency. The present absence of discussion around such issues – excepting the Legal Aid Board's (1996) helpful statements concerning the mediation pilot project proposals – suggests that a claim that current services are institutionally racist would not be wholly unwarranted. Relatedly, the present preoccupation in the professional literature with mediator 'self-awareness' – being cognisant of personal and cultural bias – needs to be loosened through a revaluation of the user/consumer perspective. In other words, the question of who the mediator and, indeed, of who the mediation service, represents should assume its rightful place at the forefront of mediator discourse. A special sensitivity to the importance of this issue looks to be required of court-based services, given the perceived proximities of civil and criminal domains.

The involvement of children in mediation appears to be a key area for further research: as yet, the implications and repercussions for parents, mediators, children and settlements reached are largely unstudied. An assembly of hard data on the background characteristics of the children directly affected by mediation would provide an essential resource for such enquiries. The present dearth of knowledge in this area is stark: the involvement and representation of children in mediation have not been given sufficient weight and the fact that so little is known about the children concerned in parental disputes is singularly telling. With this in mind, the Essex study cuts a sharp profile and the data secured provides a springboard for further research in this area.

The chapter has also focused attention on some of the difficulties, especially in terms of resources, that the involvement of children in mediation would incur. In the context of current county court practice, it is hard to see how the direct participation of children could be realised without significant changes in both the present mode of operation and its resourcing: a transformation, rather than an addendum, would appear to be required.

Finally, it is difficult to avoid the development of a deep sense of unease about the experiences and needs of children involved in family dissolution, and about the availability and quality of services currently available to assist and to counsel such children. A greater inclusion of children in mediation could act as one important way of assessing and addressing their needs, with mediators undertaking a key role in referring the child to appropriate sources of help, although a considerable shift in practice would be required before this would be possible in the realm of county court mediation.

# 7 Conclusion: Future Family Mediation

This book has been written at the most significant turning point in the history of county court family mediation in England and Wales, and, as a consequence, predicting the future feels even more unsafe than usual. Nevertheless, the preceding chapters have produced a range of key issues and questions that will undoubtedly be of importance to everyone concerned with the governance, management and delivery of mediation services, especially, although not exclusively, within the county court context. This final chapter highlights a handful of what appear to be the most pressing matters currently facing family mediation, mindful of the imminent arrival of CAFCASS and of broader shifts in the field of civil justice.

## The Persistence of Settlement as a Measure of Success

In the context of a settlement rate of approximately 70 per cent, the finding from the Essex study that about one half of all agreements made were still intact, six months after mediation, is evidently of enormous significance, not least because the persistence of settlements made at mediation has largely been ignored in both professional and research literatures. Mediators customarily say that implementing the agreement must be the responsibility of parents, while researchers have either accepted the professional agenda or avoided the issue of whether or not settlements last because of conceptual or methodological difficulties. As discussed in chapter 2, the rate of settlement is widely accepted as a worthy measure of success, while little if any concern has been afforded to whether or not agreements endure, or to how long they last. This position is clearly untenable, especially in view of the finding that many settlements break down shortly after mediation – nearly eight out of every ten agreements made in Essex county courts that failed to stand the test of time broke down within three months.

If it could be demonstrated by further empirical study that, nationally, some 50 per cent of county court settlements remain intact for a period of six months, there would be considerable cause for celebration within the mediation field. Given the level of conflict often apparent between parties in dispute, such would be no mean achievement. The efficiency of the work might also be rightly commended: after all, the mediation meeting lasts little more than an hour, often less, and therefore requires only modest resourcing. Other than, perhaps, to review the practice of employing more than one mediator per session, it is difficult to see how cost might be reduced.

Mediators, their managers and governors, and future researchers have three main indicators of performance at their disposal, in addition to a suitable measure of cost, they are: settlement rate, intactness of agreement and user satisfaction rating. From the user or consumer perspective, these evaluatory criteria are of central interest: the vast majority of parents in dispute want to reach agreement, they want settlements to last and, self-evidently, they want mediation services to be satisfactory, in terms of both process and outcome. Researchers might want to explore the relationships between the three indicators, especially the sensitivity of the intactness variable to changes in the settlement rate – it might reasonably be predicted that very high rates of agreement would be associated with lower expectations of persistence.

## More Formality, More Intervention: More Control?

Thinking of mediation as one particular expression of a much more widespread movement towards informalism has considerable theoretical merit, although there are pitfalls for the unwary – for example, formal aspects of the 'new' approaches to resolving disputes may be overlooked (Roach Anleu, 2000, p.129). The rapid growth and popularity of informalism may have also made it more difficult for the various advantages of 'formality' to be fully appreciated. The relative formality of mediation executed on court premises by family court practitioners, for example, may grant a helpful gravity and sense of occasion to proceedings. Similarly, providing a written statement of the mediated agreement and having it confirmed in some way by the district judge would be welcomed by many parents. When asked what they would wish to change about mediation, Essex parents wanted the agreement to be made more 'official' and 'enforceable'. In other words, a shift (back) to formalism was required. The characteristic reply from mediators is that parents need to make the agreement work themselves, without external intervention, and it may now be appropriate for some re-appraisal of this position to be undertaken, in the light of such strong user opinion to the contrary. There must surely be room for some form of intermediary practice between, on the one hand making a court order where no agreement is possible, and, on the other, relying entirely on the parents' management of a mediated settlement. The finding that many agreements break down quickly after mediation also adds considerable weight to the argument for some form of additional assistance to be provided to parents. Expecting them to carry all of the responsibility appears unrealistic.

A key principle of family mediation is that mediators 'control the process of mediation but not the outcome' (Parkinson, 1997, p.14). In other words, the role is concerned with establishing and maintaining an environment in which parties can resolve their dispute, rather than offering solutions. However, there may be grounds to suggest that this understanding of the role may be idealistic or incomplete. For one thing, 'outcome' and 'process' may not be as cleanly separable as they would need to be. How, for example, might a mediator's processual intervention aimed at remedying a perceived power imbalance between the two parties affect the outcome of the meeting? Secondly, there are likely to be significant differences between the mediator's role across the various types and organisations of mediation. Long-term mediation, for example, may provide far greater opportunity for mediators to perform a purely process-oriented function, simply because the pressure of time is less. By contrast, county court mediation, operating on a single session basis, may encourage a more authoritative mode in which family court officers, mindful of judicial precedent and spurred by performance targets set by. their managers, do help shape the terms of agreements. This is not to say that county court mediators are likely to be directive in a heavy-handed way, rather that they may encourage particular routes towards resolution that carry dimensions of both outcome and process.

An important criticism of 'mediation as informalism' is that it provides a camouflage for the extension of state control. New ways of dealing with disputes are developed but these lie within the shadow of judicial institution and pay ready homage to centralised power. County court mediation certainly fits this description: there is already a close proximity to the formal system at a local level and the arrival of CAFCASS promises a more direct connection with the centre. However, the notion of 'mediation as extended social control' looks to have its own problems and, even if the idea could be shown to offer some explanatory potential, the finding that many parents in dispute desire a more authoritative, interventionist mode suggests that more control would not necessarily be unwarranted. The limitations of an account founded on the simplistic dichotomization of state and society are all too readily apparent, whereas a pluralist conceptualisation would appear to offer a much greater sophistication. As discussed in chapter 5, there are long-standing tensions between the worlds of mediation, legal representation and adjudication. Sharp differences in legitimate, expert and referent power exist between the various stakeholder groups, 'balances of power' that may be sensitive to changes in central control and that, arguably, may periodically require some measure of adjustment. The divorce process has traditionally been run by lawyers and the rapid elevation of mediation has not been universally applauded within the legal profession. The users of mediation services have largely remained unheard and unmobilised, although organisations such as 'Families Need Fathers' have recently begun to take a more focused, albeit partisan, interest in mediation (Berry, 2001). The children of mediation have received minimal attention (see 'The Needs and Rights of Children', below). Against this diverse and irregular backcloth, the idea of an 'extension of state control' begs and raises a host of questions. Regulation might be seen, for example, as a way of enhancing the power of service users through the provision of, *inter alia*, standards of good practice, while mediators might experience some diminution in power. The emergence of CAFCASS might itself be regarded as an opportunity to redress present imbalances of power within the family court arena: Kroll (1998), for example, argues that:

> A new service could therefore constitute a bold move in the direction of recognising the rights and needs of children in relation to the consequences of family breakdown, however this may have come about (p.224),

and, finally, the ending of organisational linkage with the probation service might be analysed in terms of changes in the amount and expression of central control.

The possibility that mediation might prove to be a helpful factor in the control of public expenditure has made it attractive to successive governments. However, there is no conclusive evidence that, overall, mediation is the more cost-effective option: Davis (1999, p.632), for example, on the basis of research commissioned by the Legal Aid Board to monitor the introduction of publicly funded mediation, demonstrates the sensitivity of the cost of services to the number of cases being processed. It is also important to include the additional legal advice provided to parents using mediation in cost calculations. On this latter point, it is fair to say that the extra cost to non-legally aided parents may be very high – many participants in the Essex study made reference to the expense, with some quoting payments running to thousands of pounds over the period of time before, during and after mediation.

Public funding for family mediation was introduced by Part III of the *Family Law Act 1996* and, although this part of the Act was later repealed by the *Access to Justice Act 1999*, its substance has been incorporated into the Legal Services Commission's Funding Code for the Community Legal Service.

## Going it Alone: The Unrepresented Parent at Mediation

The finding that about one quarter of parents reaching agreement at county court mediation in Essex, 1998–1999, did so without being legally represented raises a number of important concerns around the establishment of fairness and contemporary mediator practice. If repeated nation-wide, and there is no obvious reason to suggest that Essex is markedly different from many other areas in this regard, then the implications for mediation and the challenge for its new governing agency would indeed be considerable. It is self-evident that mediators need to be aware of the likely effects of only one party being represented on the quality and dynamics of the meeting. The hard question is what might actually be done to ensure a balance of power in such circumstances. Of course, this issue of representation needs to be addressed much more widely within the family court arena, given the accepted wisdom that divorce without a lawyer is a somewhat perilous undertaking.

Lawyers have an important role to play in mediation and it is fair to argue that, as a rule, their presence during sessions is welcomed by parents. However, legal representation is not universally favoured: some parents, who could afford a lawyer, nevertheless choose to proceed without one on the grounds that they are sufficiently equipped to put their own case and/or that the involvement of a legal representative would, in some way, be detrimental. Mediators need to be sensitive to such feelings and decisions, although there must be a strong argument for all parents to be counselled on the disadvantages of not being legally represented. Surprisingly little attention has been given to this issue in the literature to date, despite the widespread recognition that mediators frequently encounter and attempt to shift imbalances of power. Parkinson (1997) recommends that:

> Where one partner has – or claims to have – more knowledge of the legal position, the mediator should seek to redress the balance by encouraging the other one to take legal advice before the next mediation meeting (p.245),

although the usefulness of this precept may be particularly limited for county court practitioners, who customarily employ a single mediation session per case.

## Mediation and Violence

As expressed in chapter 4 of this work, many women who attend county court mediation face the prospect of intimidation and the need for change in current practices, such as the use of shared waiting areas and confrontational seating arrangements, looks to be a priority for CAFCASS to address. There are signs that the presumption in favour of contact is beginning to be questioned in cases where intimate partner violence has taken place (Association of Chief Officers of Probation, 1998; Mosley, 2000) and the recent report from the Advisory Board on Family Law (2000) may provide further momentum.

The specific issue of mediation and violence deserves to be afforded a great deal more attention than it has so far been given.

Mediators are charged with the responsibility of providing an environment in which both parties feel able to participate in discussions about their children. This would seem to require an enhanced sensitivity, both to the general power imbalance between men and women in society and to the longitudinal nature and effects of intimate partner intimidation and abuse. A reconceptualisation of abuse as 'process', rather than 'event', would appear to be an important first step, while a review of the mediator's maxim of impartiality in this context may necessitate a rather more protracted and arduous journey.

The present view that mediation may sometimes be employed in cases involving intimate partner violence on the grounds that settlements can be reached in such circumstances looks ripe for review. Specifically, the persistence of settlements achieved in these cases needs to be studied and, if it were to be shown that such agreements were less robust over time, then the move towards the establishment of policies and practices, driven by the principle of safety, might be considerably accelerated.

On a personal note, I want to record my own sensitisation, through the course of undertaking the Essex study research, to the problems faced by women in this context. The following words, previously quoted in chapter 4, from a woman who had been terrorised by her ex-partner carry a special poignancy:

> I ran into the toilets when I heard my ex-husband's voice and stayed there until proceedings began,

and it is difficult to see how on earth she had been able to overcome such fear in order to sit down with him in the confines of a small room and reach an agreement.

The research finds little support for the 'battered husband syndrome' (Steinmetz, 1977): for example, although about one third of male participants had found having to share a court waiting area a cause for concern, the reasons they gave were the tense atmosphere created and being obliged to see their ex-spouse with her new partner. On the basis of a large-scale survey, Mooney (2000, p.210) concludes that women are at much greater risk of violence from partners or ex-partners and that violence against men from partners or ex-partners is relatively uncommon. Mediators have to find some way of delivering individualised justice against this backcloth of social inequality.


## A New Fatherhood

The finding from the Essex study that, at time of application for a section 8 order, some 16 per cent of fathers had resided with the study child/children is higher than might be predicted from national statistics relating to lone parenting (see chapter 1). Many interpretations are possible. It might be argued, for example, that the difference is indicative of a recent increase in the phenomenon of lone father parenting after divorce or separation. Two alternative explanations would be that: (1) children return to reside with their mothers some time after mediation; and (2) that the characteristics of the study population – parents who had reached a mediated agreement – are at considerable variance with those of the relevant section of wider society.

The lack of research on resident fathers has contributed to the absence of any sharp picture of purposeful fatherhood after divorce or separation. Without such a guide, fathers, mothers, mediators and other family court personnel will continue to struggle, both with the notion of lone fathering itself, and with the idea that non-resident father contact can be more than a right. Non-resident fathers who desire a much more active involvement in bringing up their children are likely to feel marginalised by the traditional assumptions and processes of mediation and the wider family court system. On the other hand, the 'cost of contact' for women deserves far greater recognition than it presently commands. The limits imposed on a woman's opportunity to establish an independent life, with or without a new partner, are frequently dismissed by men and any 'new fatherhood' must include a sensitivity to the additional burden of care that women carry.

## The Needs and Rights of Children

Much too little is known about the specific experiences, needs and views of the children of parents involved in family mediation and, in the case of county court mediation, with its reliance on one meeting for each couple, the likelihood that the child might be more directly involved is distinctly limited. Professional opinion remains divided on the question of whether children should be included, although for older children the argument against involvement appears especially vulnerable. An important attribute of the Essex study has been the establishment of a data-base on the characteristics of the 'children of mediation', including their ages, sex, special needs, number of siblings, etceteras. The finding that about one in five study children were aged ten years or above, with slightly more than one in twenty being teenagers, indicates that considerable additional resourcing might be required should a policy of directly including children in mediation be adopted. Similarly, the fact that about one half of the mediation cases concerned more than one child – 15 per cent of cases had three or more children – suggests a great deal of additional effort on the part of mediators.

## Mediation and Ethnic Minorities

The apparent absence of information about the race and ethnic origin of people undergoing mediation stands as a considerable obstacle to practitioners, managers, policy-makers and researchers alike. Without such data, and the means of collecting it systematically, it is impossible even to begin to reply to the perfectly understandable charge that mediation services are not used, or are insufficiently accessed, by people from ethnic minority groups. Ensuring that mediation services are provided to all sections of the community appears to be a priority for the new agency CAFCASS to address. A great deal more also needs to be known about the perceptions and experiences of black people involved in dispute resolution: county court mediators may need to pay particular attention to the issue of who they are seen to represent.

## A Future for Family Mediation Post-Woolf?

If mediation began as an alternative to traditional (adversarial) ways of resolving disputes, then what might its future be if those same traditional modes became markedly less adversarial? This is an important question for family mediation to face and, indeed, a most timely enquiry, given the present changes taking place within the broad field of civil justice in England and Wales following the reforms contained in the Woolf Report of 1996. Put sharply, if litigation were to become non-adversarial, then what place might there be left for family mediation to command? One possible response would be to redefine mediation as 'therapy' and calls for such a transformation have certainly been heard (Waite, 2000). A different strategy would require the vigorous marketing of mediation as complementary, rather than antagonistic, to litigation and, again, a number of writers in the field have taken pains to do this (Parkinson, 1997).

Two further questions look to be of major significance: first, what degree of change did Woolf commend; and, second, how much change is likely to occur? On the first point, it is reasonable to conclude that the shift envisaged would have left a good deal of the traditional mode unscathed while, on the second matter, there appears to be a wider spread of opinion, with Baldwin (2000), for example, opining that:

> We are currently witnessing a period of unprecedented change throughout the administration of justice, both civil and criminal. The Woolf reforms are

sweeping through the civil justice system and, in the view of many informed commentators, they are eliminating the adversarial culture in the civil courts... (p.1)

Lord Woolf was appointed by the Lord Chancellor on 28 March 1994 to review the rules and procedures of civil courts in England and Wales. His final report, published in July 1996, was followed by the Civil Procedure Rules 1998 and subsequent practice directions and amendments. Woolf raised six primary concerns about the then current system of litigation: (1) expense; (2) the delay in reaching settlements; (3) unfairness; (4) uncertainty – the duration and cost of proceedings; (5) poor governance; and (6) the adversarial culture of civil justice (see McEwan, 2000, for an application of Woolf's ideas in the area of criminal justice).

The aim of the Woolf reforms was to remove the excesses of the adversarial approach rather than to eliminate it altogether: civil justice was to remain essentially adversarial but within a 'managed' environment, with governance from judges and an expectation that litigants would focus closely on the substance rather than the process of their dispute (Brannan *et al.*, 1999, p.12). Baldwin's above comments do not reflect this, they suggest that a much more radical change is underway. However, other writers, from within the legal profession, paint a more complicated picture. Mears (2000), for example, argues that the Woolf reforms have, at least in the early stages of litigation, resulted in an increase in costs, rather than the expected decrease. Burns (2000) takes a similar position on the question of expense but is also critical of the system of case management, especially in the county court, as being too bureaucratic. Furthermore, the same author casts doubt on claims that the reforms have reduced delays and suggests that little has been achieved in addressing the frequent disparity in resources between litigants:

> The pretence that there can be a level playing field between parties – one employing skilled and experienced lawyers and able to employ the best experts, and one unrepresented and standing alone – is a cruel deception...with the effective abolition of legal aid for the general run of cases (which has been only partially and very inadequately replaced by conditional fees), the gap between rich and poor litigants is wider than ever (p.1830).

Of course, the reason why a shift away from the traditional approach of resolving disputes had been so popular was the belief that an adversarial culture exacerbated the level of conflict between parties. It was a particular effect of that culture, rather than the culture itself, that generated a search for an alternative way of reaching settlement. This is a useful point to make because it prompts an evaluation of the full range of changes driven by the Woolf reforms, in terms of their effects on the relationship between parties. So, for instance, if it is true that costs have risen and that delays have become even more protracted, then it would not be unreasonable to argue that levels of conflict have not necessarily been reduced.

Another significant feature of the new approach to civil justice is the encouraging of parties in dispute to focus closely on the 'issues'. Judges are given a key role in ensuring that litigants proceed as speedily as possible to settlement and that court rules are strictly adhered to. This is seen as providing a key departure from the adversarial approach that allowing litigants to 'drive' cases had produced. Of course, there are many similarities here with the preoccupations of family mediation and with the role executed by mediators. Again, it appears that litigation and mediation may have come closer to each other and, as a result, the space for mediation considerably foreshortened.

**Final Remarks**

Perhaps the most important and revealing discovery of this work has been the paucity of extant research in the field of family mediation. For such vital endeavour to be managed and delivered without access to a firm foundation of empirical findings looks impossible to justify. Widely respected convictions, including the superiority of comprehensive over child-centred mediation and of out-of-court over court-based forms, would appear to rest on insufficient evidence. CAFCASS should speedily assist in the commissioning of a broad programme of quantitative and qualitative research and, within this urgency, the call for further user study is arguably loudest. The successes and limitations of the Essex study research are offered as pointers and resources to this end.

# Bibliography

Adams, E. (1998), *Asian Survivors of Domestic Violence*, Social Work Monograph No. 166, University of East Anglia, Norwich.

Adams, J. (1996), 'Lone Fatherhood', *Practice*, vol. 8, no. 1, pp. 15–26.

Adelman, R., Lachs, M. and Breckman, R. (1999), 'Elder Abuse and Neglect', in R. Ammerman and M. Hersen (eds), *Assessment of Family Violence: A Clinical and Legal Sourcebook*, John Wiley and Sons, New York, pp. 271–86.

Adler, P. and Barnes, B. (1983), 'Mediation and Lawyers: The Pacific Bar Way', *Hawaii Bar Journal*, vol. 18, pp. 37–52.

Advisory Board on Family Law (2000), *Children Act Sub-Committee, A Report to the Lord Chancellor on the Question of Parental Contact in Cases Where There is Domestic Violence*, HMSO, London.

Allen, W. and Connor, M. (1997), 'An African American Perspective on Generative Fathering', in A. Hawkins and D. Dollahite (eds), *Generative Fathering: Beyond Deficit Perspectives*, Sage, Thousand Oaks, California, pp. 52–70.

Arendell, T. (1995), *Fathers and Divorce*, Sage, London.

Ashworth, A. (1995), 'Domestic Violence, Children's Safety and Family Court Welfare Practice', *Probation Journal*, vol. 42, no. 2, pp. 91–4.

Ashworth, A. (1997), 'Re-thinking Domestic Violence: Where Next in Family Court Welfare Practice?', *Probation Journal*, vol. 44, no. 3, pp. 139–43.

Association of Chief Officers of Probation (1996), *Position Statement on Domestic Violence*, ACOP, London.

Association of Chief Officers of Probation (1998), *Domestic Violence and Contact Arrangements*, ACOP, London.

Attala, M., Bauza, K., Pratt, H. and Viera, D. (1995), 'Integrative Review of Effects on Children of Witnessing Domestic Violence', *Issues in Comprehensive Paediatric Nursing*, vol. 18, pp. 163–72.

Bachman, R. (1999), 'Epidemiology of Intimate Partner Violence and Other Family Violence Involving Adults', in R. Ammerman and M. Hersen (eds), *Assessment of Family Violence: A Clinical and Legal Sourcebook*, John Wiley and Sons, New York, pp. 107–23.

Backett, K. (1987), 'The Negotiation of Fatherhood', in C. Lewis and M. O'Brien (eds), *Reassessing Fatherhood*, Sage, London.

Baldwin, J. (2000), *Annual Report 1999–2000*, Institute of Judicial Administration, School of Law, University of Birmingham, Birmingham.

Barrow, C. (1996), *Family in the Caribbean: Themes and Perspectives*, Randle, Kingston, Jamaica.

Baydar, N. (1988), 'Effects of Parental Separation and Re-entry into Union on the Emotional Well-Being of Children', *Journal of Marriage and the Family*, vol. 50, pp. 967–81.

Bender, W. (1994), 'Joint Custody: The Option of Choice', *Journal of Divorce and Re-marriage*, vol. 1, pp. 115–31.

Bennett, V. (2000), 'What's Love Got Do With It', *The Times*, 2 December 2000.

Berry, T. (2001), letters page, *The Times*, 11 January.

Biller, H. and Kimpton, J. (1997), "The Father and the School-Aged Child', in M.E. Lamb (ed), *The Role of the Father in Child Development*, John Wiley and Sons, New York, pp. 143–61.

Bitel, M. and Rolls, D. (2000), 'Mediation in a South London Secondary School', in M. Liebmann (ed), *Mediation in Context*, Jessica Kingsley, London, pp. 69–84.

Blackstone, T. (1990), *Prisons and Penal Reform*, Chatto and Windus, London.

Blankenhorn, D. (1995), *Fatherless America: Confronting our Most Urgent Social Problem*, Basic Books, New York.

Bordow, S. and Gibson, J. (1994), *Evaluation of the Family Court Mediation Service*, Family Court of Australia Research and Evaluation Unit.

Bozett, F. and Hanson, S. (eds) (1991), *Fatherhood and Families in Cultural Context*, Springer, New York.

Bradshaw, J. (1999), *Absent Fathers?* Routledge, London.

Bradshaw, J. and Miller, J. (1991), *Lone Parent Families in the UK*, HMSO, London.

Bradshaw, J., Middleton, S. and Gordon, D. (2000), *Poverty and Social Exclusion in Britain*, Joseph Rowntree Foundation, York.

Brannan, J., Ching, J., French, D., Jones, P., Napier, M., Osborne, C. & Sime, S. (1999), *Blackstone's Guide to the Civil Procedure Rules*, Blackstone, London.

Bretherton, H. (1979), 'Court Welfare Work: Practice and Theory', *Probation Journal*, vol. 26, no. 3, pp. 74–80.

Brown, C. (1994), 'The Impact of Divorce on Families', *Family and Conciliation Courts Review*, vol. 32, pp. 149–67.

Brownlee, I. (1998), *Community Punishment: A Critical Introduction*, Longman, London.

Bryan, P.E. (1994), 'The Lawyer's Role in Divorce Mediation', *Family Law Quarterly*, vol. 28, no. 2, pp. 177–222.

Burger, W. (1982), 'Isn't There a Better Way?', *American Bar Association Journal*, vol. 68, p. 274.

Burgess, A. (1997), *Fatherhood Reclaimed: The Making of the Modern Father*, Vermilion, London.

Burgess, A. and Ruxton, S. (1996), *Men and Their Children: Proposals for Public Policy*, Institute for Public Policy Research, London.

Burghes, L., Clarke, L. and Cronin, N. (1997), *Fathers and Fatherhood in Britain*, Family Policy Studies Centre, London.

Burns, R. (2000), 'A View From the Ranks', *New Law Journal*, vol. 150, no. 6963, pp. 1829–30.

Burton, S., Regan, L. and Kelly, L. (1998), *Supporting Women and Challenging Men: Lessons From the Domestic Violence Intervention Project*, Policy Press, Bristol.

Butlin, I. (2000), 'Outcome Measures in All Issues Mediation', *Family Law*, vol. 30, pp. 212–15.

Cameron, J. (1991), 'Worthy of Trust?', *Probation Journal*, vol. 38, no. 1, 38–9.

Cantwell, B., Roberts, J. and Young, V. (1998), 'Presumption of Contact in Private Law: An Interdisciplinary Issue', *Family Law*, vol. 28, pp. 226–32.

Cattanach, A. (2000), 'Working With Children Who Have Been Subjected to Violence', in H. Kemshall and J. Pritchard (eds), *Good Practice in Working with Victims of Violence*, Jessica Kingsley, London, pp. 62–74.

Cavadino, M. and Dignan, J. (1997), *The Penal System: An Introduction*, Sage, London.

Cheetham, J., Fuller, R., McIvor, G. and Petch, A. (1992), *Evaluating Social Work Effectiveness*, Open University Press, Birmingham.

Child Abuse Studies Unit (1993), *Abuse of Women and Children: A Feminist Response*, University of North London Press.

Children and Family Court Advisory Support Service (2000), *Newsletter No. 5*, CAFCASS, London.

Civil Procedure Rules (1998), SI 1998/3132 (L.17), HMSO, London.

Clerke, R. (2000), 'Mediation and Legal Help', *Family Law*, vol. 30, pp. 574–75.

Cockett, M. and Tripp, J. (1994), *The Exeter Family Study*, University of Exeter, Exeter.

Conciliation Project Unit (1989), *Report to the Lord Chancellor on the Costs and Effectiveness of Conciliation in England and Wales*, Lord Chancellor's Department, London.

Cretney, S.M. (2000), *Family Law*, Sweet and Maxwell, London.

Daly, K. (1993), 'Reshaping Fatherhood: Finding the Models', *Journal of Family Issues*, vol. 14, no. 4, pp. 510–30.

Daniels, C. (1998), *Lost Fathers: The Politics of Fatherlessness in America*, Macmillan, Basingstoke.

Davies, D. and Neal, C. (1996), *Pink Therapy: A Guide for Counsellors and Therapists Working with Lesbian, Gay and Bisexual Clients*, Open University Press, Buckingham.

Davies, H. (1994), *Guidelines for Consumer Research in the Probation Service*, West Midlands Probation Service, Birmingham.

Davis, G. (1983), 'The Inter-Departmental Committee on Conciliation: A Negative Report in Every Sense', *Probation Journal*, vol. 30, no. 4, pp. 133–5.

Davis, G. (1988), *Partisans and Mediators: The Resolution of Divorce Disputes*, Clarendon Press, Oxford.

Davis, G. (1998), 'What Works in Family Court Welfare', *Probation Journal*, vol. 45, no. 2, pp. 87–91.

Davis, G. (1999), 'Monitoring Publicly Funded Mediation', *Family Law*, vol. 29, pp. 625–35.

Davis, G. and Pearce, J. (1999), 'The Hybrid Practitioner', *Family Law*, vol. 29, pp. 547–55.

Davis, G. and Roberts, M. (1988), *Access to Agreement*, Open University Press, Milton Keynes.

De'Ath, E. (ed) (1996), *Families in Transition: Keeping in Touch When Families Part*, Stepfamily Publications, London.

DeMaris, A. and Grief, G. (1997), 'Single Custodial Fathers and Their Children: When Things Go Well', in A. Hawkins and D. Dollahite (eds), *Generative Fathering: Beyond Deficit Perspectives*, Sage, Thousand Oaks, California, pp. 134–46.

Dennis, N. (1993), *Families Without Fatherhood*, IEA Health and Welfare Unit, London.

Department of Health (1991), *Patient's Charter: Raising the Standard* (1991), HMSO, London.

Department of Health, Home Office, Lord Chancellor's Department and Welsh Office (1998), *Support Services in Family Proceedings: Future Organisation of Court Welfare Services: Consultation Paper*, Department of Health, London.

Depner, C., Cannata, K. and Ricci, I. (1994), 'Client Evaluation of Mediation Services', *Family and Conciliation Courts Review*, vol. 32, pp. 306–25.

Depner, C., Cannata, K. and Ricci, I. (1995), 'Report 4: Mediated Agreements on Child Custody and Visitation: 1991 California Family Court Services Snapshot Study', *Family and Conciliation Courts Review*, vol. 33, pp. 87–91.

Dienhart, A. (1998), *Reshaping Fatherhood: The Social Construction of Shared Parenting*, Sage, London.

Dillon, P. and Emery, R. (1996), 'Divorce Mediation and Resolution of Child Custody Disputes: Long-Term Effects', *American Journal of Orthopsychiatry*, vol. 66, p. 131.

Dixon, L. (1998), 'Re-thinking Domestic Violence; Which Way Now?', *Probation Journal*, vol. 45, no. 2, pp. 92–4.

Doherty, W. (1997), 'The Best of Times and the Worst of Times: Fathering as a Contested Arena of Academic Discourse', in A. Hawkins and D. Dollahite (eds), *Generative Fathering: Beyond Deficit Perspectives*, Sage, Thousand Oaks, California, pp. 217–27.

Dominelli, L. (1997), *Anti-Racist Social Work: A Challenge for White Practitioners and Educators*, Macmillan, Basingstoke.

Donahey, M. (1995), 'Seeking Harmony', *Journal of the Chartered Institute of Arbitrators*, vol. 61, no. 4, pp. 279–83.

Donnellan, C. (1993), *One-Parent Families: Issues for the Nineties*, Independence Educational Publishers, London.

Dowling, E. and Gorell-Barnes, G. (2000), *Working with Children and Parents Through Separation and Divorce*, Macmillan, Basingstoke.

Ehrensaft, D. (1995), 'Bringing In Fathers: The Reconstruction of Mothering', in J. Shapiro, M. Diamond and M. Greenberg (eds), *Becoming a Father: Contemporary, Social, Developmental and Clinical Perspectives*, Springer, New York, pp. 43–59.

Elliot, J., Richards, M. and Warwick, H. (1993), *The Consequences of Divorce for the Health and Well-being of Adults and Children*, Centre for Family Research, Cambridge.

Ermisch, J. (2000), 'Patterns of Household and Family Formation', in R. Berthoud and J. Gershuny (eds), *Seven Years in the Life of British Families*, Policy Press, University of Bristol, pp. 21–44.

Everitt, A., Hardiker, P., Littlewood, J. and Mullender, A. (1992), *Applied Research for Better Practice*, Macmillan, Basingstoke.

Family and Community Dispute Research Centre (1991), *Longitudinal Study of the Impact of Different Divorce Processes on Post-Divorce Relationships Between Parents and Children, Report to the Fund for Research on Dispute Resolution.*

Family Policy Studies Centre (2000), *Family Change: Guide to the Issues: Family Briefing Paper 12*, FPSC, London.

Finer Committee (1974), *Report of the Committee on One-Parent Families*, Cm 5629.

Fisher, M. (ed) (1983), *Speaking of Clients*, Joint Unit for Social Service Research: University of Sheffield, Sheffield.

Freeman, M. (1996), *The Family Law Act 1996*, Sweet and Maxwell, London.

Fuller, R. and Petch, A. (1995), *Practitioner Research*, Open University Press, Buckingham.

Furstenberg, F., Morgan, S. and Allison, P. (1987), 'Paternal Participation and Children's Well-Being After Marital Dissolution', *American Sociological Review*, vol. 52, pp. 695–701.

Gibson, J. (1992), *Custodial Fathers and Access Patterns, Family Court Research Report No. 10*, Family Court of Australia, Office of the Chief Executive, Sydney.

Gilligan, C. (1982), *In a Different Voice: Psychological Theory and Women's Development*, Harvard University Press, Cambridge.

Gould, J. and Gunther, R. (1993), *Reinventing Fatherhood*, TAB Books, Blue Ridge Summit.

Grainger, I. and Fealy, M. (1999), *Introduction to the New Civil Procedure Rules*, Cavendish, London.

Grbich, C. (1995), 'Male Primary Caregivers and Domestic Labour: Involvement or Avoidance?', *Journal of Family Studies*, vol. 1, no. 2, pp. 114–29.

Green, L. and Lewis, F. (1986), *Measurement and Evaluation in Health Education*, Mayfield, Palo Alto, California.

Hartop, B. (1996), *Peer Mediation as an Expression of Education for Mutual Understanding: Facilitating Change, Annual Report 1995–1996*, The EMU Promoting School Project, Londonderry.

Hawkins, A. and Dollahite, D. (eds) (1997), *Generative Fathering: Beyond Deficit Perspectives*, Sage, Thousand Oaks, California.

Hay, E., Hay, W. and James, A. (1992), 'Measuring the Effectiveness of Court Welfare Work', *Probation Journal*, vol. 39, no. 3, pp. 148–51.

Haynes, J. (1993), *Alternative Dispute Resolution: The Fundamentals of Family Mediation*, Old Bailey Press, Horsmonden.

Henry, S. and Milovanovic, D. (1996), *Constitutive Criminology: Beyond Postmodernism*, Sage, London.

Heron, J. (1977), *Dimensions of Facilitator Style*, Human Potential Resource Group, University of Surrey, Surrey.

Hester, M. and Radford, L. (1996), *Domestic Violence and Child Contact Arrangements in England and Denmark*, Policy Press, Bristol.

Hester, M., Pearson, C. and Radford, L. (1997), *Domestic Violence: A National Survey of Court Welfare and Voluntary Sector Mediation*, Policy Press and Joseph Rowntree Foundation, Bristol.

Hetherington, E. and Stanley-Hogan, M. (1997), 'The Effects of Divorce on Fathers and Their Children', in M. Lamb (ed), *The Role of the Father in Child Development*, John Wiley and Sons, New York, pp. 191–211.

Hill, D. (2000a), 'In Search of New Dad', *The Guardian*, 14 June.

Hill, M. (ed) (2000), 'Effective Ways of Working with Children and Their Families', *Research Highlights in Social Work*, vol. 35, Jessica Kingsley, London.

Holdaway, S. and Mantle, G. (1992), 'Policy-making in the Probation Service', in P. Carter, T. Jeffs and M. Smith (eds), *Changing Social Work and Welfare*, Open University Press, Buckingham, pp. 203–14.

Home Office (1994), *National Standards for Probation Service Family Court Welfare Work*, Home Office, London.

Home Office (1998), *Criminal Statistics for England and Wales, 1997*, Cm 4162, Home Office, London.

Home Office (2000), *Reducing Domestic Violence: What Works?: Assessing and Managing the Risk of Domestic Violence*, Briefing Note, Home Office, London.

Hosley, C. and Montemayor, R. (1997), 'Fathers and Adolescents', in M.E. Lamb (ed), *The Role of the Father in Child Development*, John Wiley and Sons, New York, pp. 162–78.

Howarth, P. (ed) (1997), *Fatherhood: An Anthology of New Writing*, Gollancz, London.

Howe, D. (1987), *An Introduction to Social Work Theory*, Wildwood House, Aldershot.

Howe, D. (1990), 'The Client's View in Context', in P. Carter *et al.* (eds), *Social Work and Social Welfare Yearbook 2*, Open University Press, Buckingham.

Hudson, W. (1990), *Partner Abuse Scale: Physical*, Walmyr, Tempe, Arizona.

Irving, H. and Benjamin, R. (1992), 'An Evaluation of Process and Outcome in a Private Mediation Service', *Mediation Quarterly*, vol. 10, pp. 35–55.

Irving, H. and Benjamin, M. (1995), *Family Mediation: Contemporary Issues*, Sage, London.

Irwin, S. (1999), 'Resourcing the Family: Gendered Claims and Obligations and Issues of Explanation', in E.B. Silva and C. Smart (eds), *The New Family?* Sage, London, pp. 31–45.

Johnson, N. (1995), 'Domestic Violence: An Overview', in P. Kingston and B. Penhale (eds), *Family Violence and the Caring Professions*, Macmillan, Basingstoke, pp. 101–26.

Johnston, J. and Campbell, L. (1993), 'Parent-Child Relationships in Domestic Violence Families Disputing Custody', *Family and Conciliation Courts Review*, vol. 31, no. 3, pp. 283–98.

Jones, A. (1999), 'The Family Courts: Does the Future Work?', *Probation Journal*, vol. 46, no. 4, pp. 253–55.

Judge, K. and Soloman, M. (1993), 'Public Opinion and the National Health Service: Patterns and Perspectives in Consumer Satisfaction', *Journal of Social Policy*, vol. 22, no. 3, pp. 299–327.

Jukes, A. (1999), *Men Who Batter Women*, Routledge, London.

Kandel-Englander, E. (1997), *Understanding Violence*, Lawrence Erlbaum Associates, Mahwah, New Jersey.

Kelly, J. (1989), 'Mediated and Adversarial Divorce: Respondent Perceptions of Their Processes and Outcomes', *Mediation Quarterly*, No. 24, pp. 71–88.

Kelly, J. (1990), *Mediated and Adversarial Divorce Resolution Processes: An Analysis of Post-Divorce Outcomes, Final Report to the Fund for Dispute Resolution*.

Kelly, J. (1991), 'Parent Interactions After Divorce: Comparison of Mediated and Adversarial Divorce Processes', *Behavioural Science and Law*, vol. 9, p. 387.

Kelly, J. and Duryee, M. (1992), 'Women's and Men's Views of Mediation in Voluntary and Mandatory Settings', *Family and Conciliation Courts Review*, vol. 30, pp. 43–9.

Kilpatrick, D. (1993), 'Rape and Other Forms of Sexual Assault', *Journal of Interpersonal Violence*, vol. 8, no. 2, pp. 193–7.

Kissman, K. and Allen, J. (1993), *Single Parent Families*, Sage, Newbury Park, California.

Kitson, G. and Holmes, W. (1992), *Portrait of Divorce: Adjustment to Marital Breakdown*, Guilford, New York.

Kline Pruett, M. and Jackson, T.D. (1999), 'The Lawyer's Role During the Divorce Process: Perceptions of Parents, Their Young Children, and Their Attorneys', *Family Law Quarterly*, vol. 33, no. 2, pp. 283–310.

Knapp, J. (1998), 'The Impact of Children Witnessing Violence', *Pediatric Clinics of North America*, vol. 45, no. 2, pp. 355–65.

Koch, T. (1992), 'A Review of Nursing Quality Assurance', *Journal of Advanced Nursing*, vol. 17, pp. 785–94.

Kraemer, S. (1995), 'What Are Fathers For?', in C. Burck and B. Speed (eds), *Gender, Power and Relationships*, Routledge, London.

Kroll, B. (1998), 'Three Children in Search of a Parent', *Probation Journal*, vol. 45, no. 4, 223–5.

Kruk, E. (1989), *Impact of Divorce on Non-Custodial Fathers: Psychological and Structural Factors Contributing to Disengagement*, Ph.D. thesis, University of Edinburgh, Edinburgh.

Kuh, D. and Maclean, M. (1990), 'Women's Childhood Experience of Parental Separation and Their Subsequent Health and Socioeconomic Status in Adulthood', *Journal of Biosocial Science*, vol. 22, pp. 121–35.

Lamb, M.E. (1997), 'The Development of Father-Infant Relationships', in M.E. Lamb (ed), *The Role of the Father in Child Development*, John Wiley and Sons, New York, pp. 104–20.

Larrabee, M. (ed) (1993), *An Ethic of Care: Feminist and Interdisciplinary Perspectives*, Routledge, London.

Law Commission (1990), *Family Law: The Ground for Divorce*, Law Commission No. 192, London.

Law Society of England and Wales (1997), *Family Mediation Code of Practice*, The Law Society, London.

Lawrence, E. (2000), 'Conflict Resolution and Peer Mediation in Primary Schools', in M. Liebmann (ed), *Mediation in Context*, Jessica Kingsley, London, pp. 53–68.

Legal Aid Board (1996), *Family Mediation Pilot Project Proposals*, Legal Aid Board, London.

Lewis, C. (1997), 'Fathers and Preschoolers', in M.E. Lamb (ed), *The Role of the Father in Child Development*, John Wiley and Sons, New York, pp. 121–42.

Lewis, C. and O'Brien, M. (eds) (1987), *Reassessing Fatherhood: New Observations on Fathers and the Modern Family*, Sage, London.

Liebmann, M. (1998), 'Mediation', in Y. Craig (ed), *Advocacy, Counselling and Mediation in Casework*, Jessica Kingsley, London, pp. 45–62.

Liebmann, M. (ed) (2000), *Mediation in Context*, Jessica Kingsley, London.

Loeb, L.L. (1999), 'New Forms of Resolving Disputes', *Family Law Quarterly*, vol. 33, no. 3, pp. 581–8.

Lindstein, T. and Meteyard, B. (1996), *What Works in Family Mediation: Mediating Residence and Contact Disputes*, Russell House, Lyme Regis.

Lipsky, M. (1980), *Street Level Bureaucracy*, Russell Sage Foundation, New York.

Lloyd, T. (1996), *What Next for Men?*, Working with Men, London.

Lord Chancellor's Department (1993), *Looking to the Future: Mediation and the Ground for Divorce: A Consultation Paper*, Cm 2424, HMSO, London.

Lord Chancellor's Department (1995), *Looking to the Future: Mediation and the Ground for Divorce: The Government's Proposals*, Cm 2799, HMSO, London.

Lord Chancellor's Department (1999), *Future Organisation of Family Court Welfare Services: Project Management Framework*, Circular, Revised 6th September 1999, Lord Chancellor's Department, London.

Lund, M. (1987), 'The Non-Custodial Father: Common Challenges in Parenting After Divorce', in C. Lewis and M. O'Brien (eds), *Reassessing Fatherhood*, Sage, London.

Lupton, D. and Barclay, L. (1997), *Constructing Fatherhood: Discourses and Experiences*, Sage, London.

Mac an Ghaill, M. (ed) (1996), *Understanding Masculinities: Social Relations and Cultural Arenas*, Open University Press, Buckingham.

Maccoby, E., Depner, C. and Mnookin, R. (1990), 'Co-parenting in the Second Year After Divorce', *Journal of Marriage and the Family*, vol. 52, pp. 141–5.

Macdonald, G., Sheldon, B. and Gillespie, J. (1992), 'Contemporary Studies of the Effectiveness of Social Work', *British Journal of Social Work*, vol. 22, no. 6, pp. 615–43.

Mahoney, M. (1991), 'Legal Issues of Battered Women: Redefining the Issue of Separation', *Michigan Law Review*, vol. 90, no. 1, pp. 1–94.

Malin, N. (ed) (2000), *Professionalism, Boundaries and the Workplace*, Routledge, London.

Mama, A. (1989), *The Hidden Struggle: Statutory and Voluntary Sector Responses to Violence Against Black Women in the Home*, The Runnymede Trust, London.

Mantle, G. (1999), *Offender Userism/Consumerism in the Probation Service of England and Wales*, Ph.D. thesis, Anglia Polytechnic University, Chelmsford.

Mantle, G. (2000), *A Consumer Survey of Agreements Reached in County Court Dispute Resolution (Mediation): Final Report to Essex Probation Service*, Anglia Polytechnic University, Chelmsford.

Mantle, G. (2001a), *County Court Dispute Resolution (Mediation)*, Occasional Paper No. 2, Essex Probation Service, Witham.

Mantle, G. (2001b), 'The Effectiveness of County Court Mediation', *Family Law*, vol. 31, pp. 147-8.

Marshall, T. and Merry, S. (1990), *Crime and Accountability: Victim Offender Mediation in Practice*, HMSO, London.

Marsiglio, W. and Cohan, M. (1997), 'Young Fathers and Child Development', in M.E. Lamb (ed), *The Role of the Father in Child Development*, John Wiley and Sons, New York, pp. 227–44.

May, L., Strikwerda, R. and Hopkins, P. (1996), *Rethinking Masculinity: Philosophical Explorations in the Light of Feminism*, Rowman and Littlefield, London.

Mayer, J. and Timms, N. (1970), *The Client Speaks: Working Class Impressions of Casework*, Routledge and Kegan Paul, London.

McCarthy, P. (2000), 'Providing Information: The Views of Professionals', *Family Law*, vol. 30, pp. 550–4.

McCarthy, P. and Walker, J. (1996), *Evaluating the Longer Term Impact of Family Mediation, Newcastle: Relate Centre for Family Studies*, University of Newcastle-upon-Tyne, Newcastle-upon-Tyne.

McEwan, J. (2000), 'Co-operative Justice and the Adversarial Criminal Trial: Lessons from the Woolf Report', in S. Doran and J. Jackson (eds), *The Judicial Role in Criminal Proceedings*, Hart, Oxford, pp. 171–81.

Mears, M. (2000), 'Woolf: The Jury is Still Out?', *New Law Journal*, vol. 150, no. 6961, p. 1731.

Mediation UK (1995), *Training Manual in Community Mediation Skills*, Mediation UK, Bristol.

Mirrlees-Black, C. (1999), *Domestic Violence: Findings From a New British Crime Survey Self-completion Questionnaire*, Research Study 191, Home Office, London.

Mitchell, A. (1985), *Children in the Middle: Living Through Divorce*, Tavistock, London.

Mooney, J. (2000), *Gender, Violence and the Social Order*, Macmillan, Basingstoke.

Moore, L. (1996), 'Lawyer Mediators: Meeting the Ethical Challenges', *Family Law Quarterly*, vol. 30, p. 679.

Morgan, C. (1996), *Mediation in West Glamorgan Family Court Welfare Service*, West Glamorgan Probation Service, Neath.

Morgan, G. (1986), *Images of Organisation*, Sage, London.

Morran, D. (1995), 'Male Offenders' Violence Against Women: Suggestions for Practice', *Probation Journal*, vol. 42, no. 4, pp. 215–9.

Mosley, S. (2000), '"Risk of Harm" and Domestic Violence: An Issue for the Family Court?', *Probation Journal*, vol. 47, no. 3, pp. 184–92.

Moss, P. (ed). (1995), *Father Figures: Fathers in the Families of the 1990s*, HMSO, Edinburgh.

Mullender, A. and Hague, G. (2000), *Reducing Domestic Violence...What Works?: Women Survivors' Views*, Briefing Note, Home Office, London.

Mullender, A. and Morley, R. (1994), *Children Living With Domestic Violence: Putting Men's Abuse of Women on the Child Care Agenda*, Whiting and Birch, London.

Murray, J. (2000), 'Paying the price of a second family', *The Times*, 18 July.

Nichols, T. (1999), 'Mediation: Section 29 and All That', *Family Law*, vol. 29, pp. 656–7.

Newman, P. (2000), 'Commercial Alternative Dispute Resolution (ADR)', in M. Liebmann (ed), *Mediation in Context*, Jessica Kingsley, London, pp. 177–90.

Office for National Statistics (ONS) (2000a), *Social Trends*, vol. 30, ONS, London.

Office for National Statistics (2000b), *Marriage, Divorce and Adoption Statistics: Review of the Registrar General on Marriage, Divorce and Adoption in England and Wales, 1998*, Series FM2 No. 26, ONS, London.

Ogus, A., Walker, J. and Jones-Lee, M. (1989), *Costs and Effectiveness of Conciliation in England and Wales: Summary of the Report of the Conciliation Project Unit*, University of Newcastle upon Tyne, Newcastle upon Tyne.

O'Leary, K. and Murphy, C. (1999), 'Clinical Issues in the Assessment of Partner Violence', in R. Ammerman and M. Hersen (eds), *Assessment of Family Violence: A Clinical and Legal Sourcebook*, John Wiley and Sons, New York, pp. 24–47.

Parke, R.D. (1996), *Fatherhood*, Harvard University Press, Cambridge, Massachusetts.

Parker, H., Sumner, M. and Jarvis, G. (1989), *Unmasking the Magistrates: the 'Custody or Not' Decision in Sentencing Young Offenders*, Open University Press, Milton Keynes.

Parkinson, L. (1997), *Family Mediation*, Sweet and Maxwell, London.

Pearson, J. and Thoennes, N. (1984), 'A Preliminary Portrait of Client Reactions to Three Court Mediation Programs', *Mediation Quarterly*, vol. 3, pp. 21–40.

Phares, V. (1998), *"Poppa" Psychology: The Role of Fathers in Children's Mental Well-Being*, Praeger, London.

Phillipson, C. and Biggs, S. (1995), 'Elder Abuse: A Critical Overview', in P. Kingston and B. Penhale (eds), *Family Violence and the Caring Professions*, Macmillan, Basingstoke, pp. 181–203.

Popay, J., Hearn, J. and Edwards, J. (1998), *Men, Gender Divisions and Welfare*, Routledge, London.

Pringle, K. (1995), *Men, Masculinities and Social Welfare*, UCL Press, London.

Ptacek, J. (1999), *Battered Women in the Courtroom: The Power of Judicial Responses*, Northeastern University Press, Boston.

Quinton, D. (1996), 'The Consequences of Contact: Implications for Adult Adjustment', in E. De'Ath (ed), *Families in Transition: Keeping in Touch When Families Part*, Stepfamily Publications, London, pp. 39–46.

Rees, S. and Wallace, A. (1982), *Verdicts on Social Work*, Edward Arnold, London.

Renzetti, C. (1992), *Violent Betrayal: Partner Abuse in Lesbian Relationships*, Sage, London.

Reynolds, C. (2000), 'Workplace Mediation', in M. Liebmann (ed), *Mediation in Context*, Jessica Kingsley, London, pp. 166–76.

Roach Anleu, S.L. (2000), *Law and Social Change*, Sage, London.

Roberts, M. (1997), *Mediation in Family Disputes: Principles and Practice*, Arena, Aldershot.

Robinson, M. (1999), 'Family Mediation Involving Children', in M. Hill (ed), *Effective Ways of Working with Children and their Families*, Jessica Kingsley, London, pp. 128–43.

Rodgers, B. and Pryor, J. (1998), *Divorce and Separation: The Outcomes for Children*, Joseph Rowntree Foundation, York.

Russell, M.N. and Frohberg, J. (1995), *Confronting Abusive Beliefs: Group Treatment for Abusive Men*, Sage, London.

Sainsbury, E. (1987), 'Client Studies: Their Contribution and Limitations in Influencing Social Work Practice', *British Journal of Social Work*, vol. 17, pp. 635–44.

Sarat, A. and Felstiner, W. (1986), 'Law and Strategy in the Divorce Lawyer's Office', *Law and Society Review*, vol. 20, p. 129.

Segal, L. (1997), *Slow Motion: Changing Masculinities, Changing Men*, Virago, London.

Seltzer, J. (1991), 'Relationships Between Fathers and Children Who Live Apart: The Father's Role After Separation', *Journal of Marriage and the Family*, vol. 53, pp. 79–101.

Sharpe, S. (1994), *Fathers and Daughters*, Routledge, London.

Shulman, S. and Seiffge-Krenke, I. (1997), *Fathers and Adolescents: Developmental and Clinical Perspectives*, Routledge, London.

Simpson, B. (1994), 'Access and Child Contact Centres in England and Wales: An Ethnographic Perspective', *Children and Society*, vol. 8, pp. 42–5

Simpson, B., McCarthy, P. and Walker, J. (1995), *Being There: Fathers After Divorce*, University of Newcastle upon Tyne, Newcastle upon Tyne.

Smart, C. (1999), 'The "New" Parenthood: Fathers and Mothers after Divorce', in E.B. Silva and C. Smart (eds), *The New Family?*, Sage, London, pp. 100–14.

Snarey, J. (1993), *How Fathers Care For the Next Generation: A Four-Decade Study*, Harvard University Press, Cambridge, Massachusetts.

Speake, S., Cameron, S. and Gilroy, R. (1997), *Young Single Fathers: Participation in Fatherhood: Barriers and Bridges*, Family Policy Studies Centre, London.

Stanko, E. (1998), 'Making the Invisible Visible: A Personal Journey', in S. Holdaway and P. Rock (eds), *Thinking About Criminology*, UCL, London, pp. 35–54.

Stanley, N. (1997), 'Domestic Violence and Child Abuse: Developing Social Work Practice', *Child and Family Social Work*, vol. 2, pp. 135–45.

Steinmetz, S. (1977), 'The Battered Husband Syndrome', *Victimology*, vol. 2, no. 3–4, pp. 499–509.

Stelman, A. (1993), 'Domestic Violence: Old Crime, Sudden Interest', *Probation Journal*, vol. 40, no. 4, pp. 193–8.

Stevenson, M. (2000), 'Family Mediation: Working to Support Separated Families', in M. Liebmann (ed), *Mediation in Context*, Jessica Kingsley, London, pp. 39–52.

Strang, H. and Braithwaite, J. (eds) (2000), *Restorative Justice: Philosophy to Practice*, Ashgate, Aldershot.

Taylor, A. and Sanchez, E. (1991), 'Out of the White Box: Adapting Mediation to the Needs of Hispanic and Other Minorities Within American Society', *Family and Conciliation Courts Review*, vol. 29, no. 2, pp. 114–27.

Vincent, J.P. and Jouriles, E.N. (eds). (2000), *Domestic Violence: Guidelines for Research-Informed Practice*, Jessica Kingsley, London.

Waite, I. (2000), 'W(h)ither Contact? An Alternative To Current Practices', *Probation Journal*, vol. 47, no. 3, pp. 203–5.

Walby, S. and Myhill, A. (2000), *Reducing Domestic Violence...What Works?: Assessing and Managing the Risk of Domestic Violence*, Briefing Note, Home Office, London.

Walker, J. (1996), 'Re-Negotiating Fatherhood', in E. De'Ath (ed), *Families in Transition: Keeping in Touch When Families Part*, Stepfamily, London, pp. 47–60.

Walker, J. and Hornick, J. (1996), *Communication in Marriage and Divorce*, BT Forum, London.

Walker, J., McCarthy, P. and Timms, N. (1994), *Mediation: The Making and Remaking of Co-operative Relationships: An Evaluation of the Effectiveness of Comprehensive Mediation*, Relate Centre for Family Studies, University of Newcastle upon Tyne, Newcastle upon Tyne.

Walklate, S. (2000), 'From the Politicization to the Politics of the Crime Victim', in H. Kemshall and J. Pritchard (eds), *Good Practice in Working with Victims of Violence*, Jessica Kingsley, London, pp. 10–19.

White, N. (1994), 'About Fathers: Masculinity and the Social Construction of Fatherhood', *Australian and New Zealand Journal of Sociology*, vol. 30, no. 2, pp. 119–131.

Wilding, P. (1982), *Professional Power and Social Welfare*, Routledge and Kegan Paul, London.

Woolf Report (1996), *Access to Justice: Final Report by Lord Woolf MR, to the Lord Chancellor on the Civil Justice System in England and Wales*, HMSO, London.

Wright, M. (1996), *Justice for Victims and Offenders*, Waterside, Winchester.

Wynne, J. (2000), 'Victim-Offender Mediation in Practice', in M. Liebmann (ed) *Mediation in Context*, Jessica Kingsley, London, pp. 126–39.

Yegge, R.E. (1994), 'Divorce Litigants Without Lawyers', *Family Law Quarterly*, vol. 28, no. 3, pp. 407–19.

Young, J. (1981), 'Thinking Seriously About Crime: Some Models of Criminology', in M. Fitzgerald, G. McLennan, and J. Pawson (eds), *Crime and Society: Readings in History and Theory*, Routledge and Kegan Paul, London, pp. 248–309.

Young, K. (1977), 'Values in the Policy Process', *Policy and Practice*, vol. 5, pp. 1–12.

# Appendix 1: The Essex Study

This is an account of the main findings and methods of a large-scale postal survey of parents and carers who had reached full agreement at county court mediation in Essex. The study was jointly funded by Anglia Polytechnic University and Essex Probation Service, 1998-2000. The aims of the research have been:

- to evaluate recipient perspectives on the significance, duration, outcomes and effects of in-court agreements; and
- to consider the potential implications for EPS policy and practice.

## Main Findings

- 52 per cent of participants said that arrangements agreed at mediation were still intact after six months. The following factors were found to be significant:

    - number of children;
    - whether or not the participant had felt able to say everything they really wanted to;
    - the level of dissatisfaction/satisfaction felt;
    - the age of the child;
    - the type of order applied for;
    - whether or not the participant had felt fairly treated during mediation.

- Of those agreements that did not last, 21 per cent had been in place less than one week, 51 per cent less than one month, and 78 per cent had lasted less than three months.

- 72 per cent of participants said that nothing else could have been done at mediation to ensure that the arrangements would have stayed intact. Most cited the attitude or actions of the 'other' parent as the reason why arrangements had changed.

- In cases where arrangements had changed, 75 per cent said that mediation had not helped to reach agreement about the new arrangements. In cases where mediation had helped, most participants felt that there had been an improvement in communication with their ex-partner.

- 84 per cent of participants reported one mediator present during the session.

- 91 per cent said that the gender or race of the mediator(s) was not an issue for them.

- 78 per cent had had no previous expectations of mediation. Where participants had expectations, the most frequent source was from previous mediation sessions.

- 76 per cent had been legally represented.

- 78 per cent thought that, in principle, having a solicitor present was a good idea.

- 74 per cent had found it helpful to have solicitors present in their own mediation session. The availability of immediate legal/ procedural advice, the support given by solicitors and the role played by the solicitor in recording the details of the agreement were all important factors.

- 79 per cent of participants had shared the Court waiting area with the other parent/party before mediation. Of those who had, 53 per cent said that it had been of concern to them. However, women (63 per cent) were more likely than men (39 per cent) to express concern.

- 68 per cent said that groundrules had been set by the mediator. Of these, 88 per cent had felt that the groundrules had been effectively applied.

- 87 per cent said that they had sat directly opposite the other parent/party during mediation. Of those who had, 72 per cent had not found this to be of concern. However, women were three times more likely to have such concerns.

- 71 per cent had felt able to say everything they really wanted to the mediator.

- 84 per cent said that, in principle, mediation was a good thing.

- 44 per cent had been very satisfied or satisfied: 26 per cent had felt their mediation session to have been 'OK' and 30 per cent had been dissatisfied or very dissatisfied. Satisfaction was more likely if:-

  - the agreement was still intact, or it had lasted a reasonable time;
  - the presence of solicitors had been helpful;
  - groundrules had been effectively applied;
  - the participant had felt able to say everything they really wanted;
  - mediation had, in principle, been seen as a good thing;
  - the participant had felt fairly treated.

- Having a structured, managed and fair opportunity to establish communication and reach agreement was seen as the best thing about mediation.

- Asked if they could change one thing what would it be, most participants wanted agreements to be binding or enforced. There were also many requests to meet with the mediator one-to-one before the session.

- 84 per cent had felt fairly treated. Of those who had felt unfairly treated: men cited assumptions made about the relative importance of fathers and mothers to their children; while women related their sense of unfairness to the 'burden of care' and to a lack of sensitivity to the issue of domestic violence and intimidation.

## Population, Sample and Research Methods

*Population and Sample: Expected and Actual*

In planning the study, a series of estimated figures for predicting the likely populations and sub-populations were employed based on corresponding numbers from previous years. The assumption was that in-court dispute resolution had been offered annually by Essex Family Courts Service to some 1200 sets of parents and, of these, about 900 sets had accepted the invitation. Mediators are expected to, and do, achieve a 70 per cent rate of 'full agreements' (630) and an 8 per cent rate of 'partial agreements' (72), leaving some 200 cases per annum wherein agreement is not reached. On this basis, the aim was to survey both parties for all full agreements achieved during the period 1 April 1998 - 31 March 1999. The sample was thus one of 'complete coverage' over the year.

However, the total number of cases notified to the research team over the stipulated time period was 448 (170 from Southend, 105 from Chelmsford, 102 from Colchester and 71 from Harlow County Court), from which 44 were subsequently excluded - 36 were duplicates, 7 had been included in the pilot/sensitisation phase of the project and one case was personally known to the researcher. Of the 404 cases remaining, a number of addresses were unavailable and some preliminary letters had been returned 'addressee gone away' via the Post Office. Some cases involved more than two parties. As a result, the total number of people (rather than cases) sent a postal questionnaire was 794. Of this cohort, 72 questionnaires were returned via the Post Office 'addressee gone away' leaving an active sample of 722 individuals.

A total of 345 completed questionnaires were returned giving a satisfactory response rate of 48 per cent. Of these returns, 100 were from applicants, 115 from respondents and 65 were from both applicant and respondent (i.e. 65 pairs = 130 individual returns). Because of the significant gap between expected (630) and actual (448) populations, the absolute number of returns is considerably lower than predicted, as is the number of 'paired' replies, i.e. from both applicant and respondent.

Nevertheless, the numbers have been sufficient for statistical analyses using the SPSS programme.

*Population Characteristics*

- 38 per cent of cases in the sample were mediated at Southend County Court; 23 per cent at Chelmsford: 23 per cent at Colchester; and 16 per cent at Harlow County Court.

- 59 per cent of applications were for contact orders; 16 per cent were for residence orders; 11 per cent for contact *plus* parental responsibility orders; and 8 per cent were for residence *plus* contact, or residence *or* contact orders; of the remainder, only contact *plus* specific issue and residence *plus* prohibited steps orders achieved more than a 1 per cent frequency.

- As would be expected, the distribution by gender is very close to 50:50: this compares with a 55:45 female to male ratio for participants, i.e. women were slightly more likely to complete and return their questionnaires than were men.

- 3.4 per cent of the sample were under 21 years of age; 13 per cent under 26; 38 per cent under 31; 65 per cent under 36; 87 per cent under 41; 95 per cent under 46; 98 per cent under 51; and 1.8 per cent were aged 51 years or more.

- 2 per cent of 'first' (i.e. a very small number of cases had more than one applicant or respondent) applicants were under 21 years of age; 11 per cent under 26; 34 per cent under 31; 61 per cent under 36; 84 per cent under 41; 94 per cent under 46; 98 per cent under 51; and 99 per cent were aged less than 56 years.

- 5 per cent of first respondents were under 21 years of age; 15 per cent under 26; 42 per cent under 31; 69 per cent under 36; 90 per cent under 41; 96 per cent under 46; and 99 per cent were aged less than 51 years.

- 77 per cent of first applicants were male.

- 78 per cent of first respondents were female.

- In 75 per cent of cases, the first applicant was the father of the eldest (or only) child: the first applicant was the mother in 22 per cent; and in 3 per cent of cases the first applicant was step-parent, grandparent or foster mother.

- In 78 per cent of cases, the first respondent was the mother of the eldest (or only) study child: the first respondent was the father in 22 per cent of cases: in less than 1 per cent of cases was the relationship other than maternal or paternal.

- 50 per cent of cases had only one child; 36 per cent had two; 12 per cent had 3: 2.5 per cent had 4 and 0.5 per cent had 5 children.

- 45 per cent of eldest (or only) study children were female and 55 per cent were male.

- In cases where there were two or more study children, 51 per cent of second children were female and 49 per cent were male.

- In 26 per cent of cases, the eldest (or only) child was under four years of age: 47 per cent under 7 years; 74 per cent under 10; 92 per cent under 13; and 99 per cent were under 16 years of age.

- In cases where there were two or more children, 24 per cent of second children were aged less than four years; 58 per cent less than 7; 87 per cent less than 10; and 98 per cent were under 13 years of age.

- In 80 per cent of cases the study child/children lived with their mother: 16 per cent with their father; 3 per cent with other family members; and only in 1 per cent of cases were study children living apart from each other.

- In 33 per cent of the cases there was at least one 'other' child residing with the applicant, respondent or elsewhere.

- 13 per cent of the cases had at least one child with a special need.

- 14 per cent of the cases had at least one child known to Social Services.

- 9 per cent of the cases had at least one child currently with a social worker involved.

- 1 per cent of cases included at least one child currently on the Child Protection Register.

- No data on race nor ethnicity was available (this is because the Court proforma 'C1' does not collect such data).

*Research Methods: Data Collection*

In order to develop a postal questionnaire for the survey, ten face-to-face interviews and six telephone interviews were undertaken with people who had reached full agreement in mediation sessions during March 1998. The face-to-face interviews were conducted in the parent's homes. In combination with insights drawn from other studies in this field, suggestions from members of the Steering Group and standard principles of survey research, this information was used to construct a draft questionnaire which was subsequently despatched to all parties who had reached agreement in Essex County Court mediations during the month of February 1998. This 'pilot' phase of the research produced a 50 per cent response rate, after a follow-up request, and allowed the design of a final mail questionnaire for use in the main data-collection phase.

A covering letter, assuring confidentiality and emphasising the independence of the research, accompanied each questionnaire and, through the assignment of a code to each schedule, it was possible to identify non-responders so as to target the follow-up invitations to participate in the project. A telephone contact, with answer machine, was provided for people wanting further information about the research.

*Research Methods: Data Analysis*

The study has produced and analysed a vast amount of quantitative and qualitative data. The questionnaire data comprises: (1) readily quantifiable information, for example the percentage of participants who said that groundrules had been set by the mediator; (2) codeable qualitative data, for example, the reasons given for changes to agreed arrangements; and (3) illustrative qualitative data, for example, information supplied by participants in response to the 'Is there anything else you would like to say?' item on the questionnaire. In addition, a large volume of background data was derived from EPS papers about the adults and children involved, plus written accounts from mediators giving details of agreements made.

All background and readily quantifiable questionnaire data were entered on the computer and subjected to statistical analysis using SPSS, a standard statistical package. Frequency distributions and cross-tabulations have been generated: the statistical significance of associations between variables has been gauged using the standard chi-square test.

Codeable qualitative data has been collated and analysed manually. The approach adopted has been to discern major and minor themes within the data, using a simple frequency count.

Paired responses have been combined with relevant background data and details of the agreements made to produce a small set of case studies (Appendix 2).

The assembly of 'paired data' (i.e. responses from both parties) was a key ambition of the study and has proven extremely important in a number of ways. It has allowed a level of confidence in the representativeness of the questionnaire data: using SPSS, it has been possible to undertake a series of comparative analyses - first, a comparison of the distributions of background characteristics and questionnaire responses made by paired participants with those of and from singleton participants; second, a comparison of background characteristics between non-participants and participants. No statistically significant differences were apparent in either comparative analysis, suggesting, although not proving, that the questionnaire data secured is likely to be representative of the views and experiences of those parents in the sample who did not return a questionnaire. Previous consumer research designs (Morgan, 1996) that were not equipped to identify 'paired' responses, nor to distinguish between applicants and respondents, are open to much sharper criticism in terms of representativeness.

A further advantage of having the paired data is that a more detailed picture of each mediation 'case' comes into view. Having both perspectives also allows a series of comparisons and contrasts to be made: this has proved of crucial importance in assessing the outcome of mediation agreements.

Interpretation of the data was assisted by a discursive meeting with Essex Family Courts practitioners and by direct observation of mediation sessions at Chelmsford County Court.

# Appendix 2: Case Studies

Six studies are presented, based on testimonies of both parents for each case, set against background information derived from files. Although the studies will be of general interest, they may be particularly useful within the contexts of training and supervision. All names of children and parents have been changed.

**Case A**

Child:    Maisie A., aged 5, lives with mother, her new partner and Maisie's half brother.

Applicant: Mr S. Father, aged 39.
Respondent: Miss A. Mother, aged 29.

Mr S has applied for a specific issue order because he wants Miss A to disclose Maisie's address, phone number, doctor and school details. A contact order is already in place, stipulating details of staying contact every other weekend, with other contact arrangements to be made by the two parties.

Before mediation, both parties had been apprehensive about the shared waiting area: Mr S was anxious about Miss A's new partner, feeling that he was blocking contact; Miss A felt that the level of tension was raised. Mr S had no particular expectations of the session while Miss A writes:

> I expected someone to listen and take note of past history...expectations based on Relate mediation sessions where both sides seemed fairly listened to and not judged or ordered.

Mr S was legally represented, Miss A was not. Mr S had felt that it had been helpful to have his solicitor present: Miss A had felt that the solicitor's presence had not been helpful. The parties had sat directly opposite each other during mediation: Mr S had not been concerned about this but Miss A had found it very difficult.

Although groundrules had been set by the mediator, Miss A writes that Mr S had been aggressive and rude, being checked at one point by his solicitor but not by the mediator. Neither party had felt able to say everything they really wanted to. Mr S explains:

> Because, if you tried to get something across they thought all you are doing is arguing, but all I want is the best for my daughter,

while Miss A writes that Mr S had dominated the conversation and that time had run out before she had had a chance to make her point. Both parties had been dissatisfied with the session. Nevertheless, agreement was reached that:

- Maisie's doctor and school details would be given to Mr S;
- Mr S to use maternal grandmother's address and phone number for contact;
- Maisie would be taken on holiday by her father for one week, details of place and time for collection and return agreed;
- Fortnightly staying contact to continue.

Both parties say that the arrangements are no longer intact, although they don't agree on how long the arrangements lasted - Mr S says one week, Miss A says six weeks. All face-to-face contact has apparently ceased. Mr S writes:

> Because in court my ex agrees with me about our daughter and when it comes to the day, she just makes excuses, i.e. phone calls once a week, extra visits while on school holidays, she had not kept to these agreements

and Miss A explains that:

> They have changed because despite my protestations at the time of mediation which were ignored, my daughter was ordered to see her father, resulting in severe emotional upset and several acute asthma attacks. She no longer sees him.

If he could change one thing about mediation, Mr S would like some way of ensuring that the agreements made are kept. Miss A says that 'parties that do not wish to meet should be kept separate.'

**Case B**

Children:  Michael B., aged 11 and Raymond B, aged 9, both living with mother. Mother remarried. No further details.

Applicant: Mr. B. father, aged 38.
Respondent: Mrs W., age unknown.

Mr B has applied for a contact order. Previous mediation had resulted in arrangements being agreed but Mr. B reports that there have been difficulties over 'flexibility' and over staying contact during school holidays.

Before mediation, Mr B had not felt concerned about the shared waiting area while Mrs W had felt nervous. Both had expectations of the session based on the previous mediation, seven months before, which had been positive. Mr B was legally represented and felt that it had been useful to have his solicitor present:

> ...an observer who you could refer to for additional advice and to confirm understanding of the agreement

while Mrs W had not been represented and had found the presence of Mr B's unhelpful:

> ...I had a feeling of being pressured by my ex-husband to agree to his terms.

Although the two parties had sat directly opposite during the session, this had caused no concern. Groundrules had been set and both parties felt that the rules had been applied effectively. Both parties felt that the session had been OK and that they had been able to say everything they really wanted to. Mr B adds:

> I felt that I had to be careful about what I said so as not to cause any offence to my ex-wife. I think that certain things need to be said but they may be considered counter-productive by the mediator, thus jeopardising any potential agreement.

Agreement was reached for:

- weekend staying contact fortnightly;
- two additional half weeks in the summer holiday and one week in the autumn half term.

Both parties say that the arrangements are still intact. If she could change one thing about mediation, Mrs W writes:

> That it could be held somewhere other than at court as it felt a little intimidating, when you are discussing your family arrangements,

while Mr B offers three suggestions:

> (1) Notes should be allowed to be taken so that there is no mis-interpretation of the agreement (detailed notes could be agreed and seen by the Judge); (2) half an hour is not long enough. One hour at least should be allowed with an option to hold further meetings if required; (3) if there is more than one session then the same mediator should be present at each (each mediator has a different opinion. I have had two sessions and each mediator handled the situation differently!).

## Case C

Children:    Emma C., aged 11 and Terence C., aged 7, both living with mother.

Applicant: Mr. C. father, aged 40.
Respondent: Mrs C., aged 37.

Mr C has applied for contact and specific issue orders, citing an apparent breakdown in arrangements made via a previous contact order and making a request for leave to take Emma and Terence on holiday. In his written application he also asks for the appointment of a court welfare officer to assess the 'children's well-being'. The two parties had not shared the court waiting area: Mrs C writes that this would have caused her concern. Mrs C had been legally represented and had found the presence of her solicitor helpful because:

> I am very intimidated and frightened by my ex-husband. It was comforting for me personally to be legally represented although I understand that my solicitor could not comment.

Mr C had not been represented and felt that, generally, their presence was not a good idea. During mediation the two parties had sat opposite to one another: Mr C had not been concerned while Mrs C writes:

My only concern is my complete nervousness in my ex-husband's presence. He only has to be in the same room as myself for me to become upset.

Mr C had not been aware of any groundrules but Mrs C comments:

The mediator was very fair, listened to both sides and made a fair judgement in my opinion. She did not allow my ex-husband to continually bully me and gave me a chance to have my say... During the session following a tirade of abuse from my husband, I became upset but the mediator was sympathetic towards me and asked my ex-husband to behave.

Overall, Mrs C had been satisfied with the session while Mr C had been very dissatisfied, although he does not offer any reason for this. Both parties had felt able to say what they wanted to. Agreement was reached for:

-   contact to resume, with date, times for collection and return;
-   contact thereafter to be agreed by two parties with Mr C informing Mrs C of his availability and plans for the particular contact period;
-   the requested holiday to be considered having ascertained the children's wishes;
-   a further mediation session in 3 months time.

Both parties agree that the arrangements are no longer intact and that all contact has ceased: Mr C says the arrangements lasted one week because:

Despite mediation and agreements made, my ex-spouse refused to comply,

while Mrs C says a few weeks, explaining that:

My ex-husband was asked to give me adequate notice of when he wanted to see the children, what activities he had planned for them for that particular contact visit, and he was asked not to take the children into the pub. All these things he has rescinded upon.

Both parties agree that nothing else could have been done at mediation to ensure that the arrangements stayed intact. Mrs C feels that leaving things up to Mr C (to tell her about his availability and plans) would never work, given his hostile attitude. For his part Mr C says that the arrangements would need to be have been enforced by the Court. He also mentions that the review mediation session had not taken place (no reason given) and that his request for further mediation had been refused by the Court on the grounds of expense.

## Case D

Children:    Peter D., aged 9, and Samuel D., aged 7. Sam has special educational needs and has been statemented.

The applicant mother, Mrs D., and respondent father, Mr D. still share the matrimonial home with Peter and Sam. Mrs D., who applied for residence orders writes:

> I had naturally presumed that the children would reside primarily with me, having good and frequent contact with their father. However, he has indicated...that he is seeking provision that the children reside equally with him. We can make no progress, including my moving out with the children because of the increasingly intolerable conditions in the family home, until it is agreed or ordered that the children will reside primarily with me.

Mr D had not expected to be successful in his wish for shared care, '...because traditionally the mother is nearly always granted custody'. Both parties had felt that mediation had gone well with groundrules set and applied effectively by the mediator. Neither had been unduly apprehensive about the shared waiting area or seating arrangements used during mediation. Both had been legally represented and, for Mrs D, the presence of her solicitor had been helpful:

> So I was not pressurised by my husband's forceful personality to agree to all his wishes against my views,

while Mr D had felt that both solicitors had:

> ...helped in taking the sting or animosity out of the situation.

The agreement was for shared care on a two-weekly programme: no order was made other than that the application would be adjourned for six months with liberty to either party to resume it, in the absence of which the application to be withdrawn. At the six months point, both parties agreed that the arrangements made for shared care were still intact.

## Case E

Children:   Louisa E., aged 6, and Steven, aged 4, both living with their mother.

Applicant: Mr E., father, aged 35.
Respondent: Mrs E., mother.

Mr E applied for a contact order, pursuant to a contact order made some twelve months previously. He writes:

> Until recently, I enjoyed staying contact with my two children at my home, on alternate weekends, Saturday to Sunday. The children's mother has now refused me staying contact with the two children, for reasons totally unfounded. I am now enjoying contact for only a few hours on alternate weekends, on Saturdays. The children's mother has also told me that I will not be exercising contact during the school holidays...

Before mediation, Mrs E had been concerned by the shared waiting area because '...I cannot stand the sight of him', while, during the session, she had a mixed reaction to the seating arrangement:

> Yes and no. He couldn't talk and look me in the eye with what he was saying....and the mediator sat at the end of the table so you have to keep turning round to talk to him.

Groundrules were set and applied effectively. Both parties were legally represented and had found the presence of solicitors helpful. Mrs E explains:

> They can observe the other party and how they act and step in when lies are told by them.

Mr E had been satisfied with the session, feeling that it had allowed an opportunity to talk without being interrupted, while Mrs E. had been dissatisfied because:

I did expect them to have at least read as to why we got divorced. It would have saved listening to stupid recommendations like 'why don't you let him in the house and have a cup of tea and chat in front of the children?'

An agreement was reached that weekend staying contact would resume, on a set date, and that two extra days would be added over the holiday break. There was no reference in the mediator's notes to arrangements for further holidays. At the six months point, both parties agree that the arrangements have held in place. The respondent mother makes references to her solicitor's bill being 'in the thousands' and ends her testimony as follows:

We are not criminals as such. Just getting divorced and fighting for the children. The Courts are cold and unfriendly places, more like a cattle market. The Judge never talks to us, most of the time, never even looks up from her paperwork. The mediation goes on and on, then when you see the Judge she doesn't even know what's happened, and the solicitors have to tell her before her decision.

## Case F

Children:   Julie F., aged 14, Janice F., aged 12 and Christine aged 4 years, all living with their mother.

Applicant: Mr F., father, aged 44.
Respondent: Ms F.

Mr F applied for a contact order on the grounds that he had been 'denied contact with the children'. Both parties had been legally represented: Mr F had been unhappy with his solicitor because '...he did not think about the children, only the finance', while Ms F had felt vulnerable in her husband's presence and thus grateful that her solicitor was included.

Groundrules had been set and applied effectively, 'extremely fair' and 'neither of us were allowed to fly off the handle' being the respective comments of applicant and respondent. Mr F had been dissatisfied with the mediation. He had felt that the mediator would not accept his request for 'reasonable contact', wanting instead to make definite (limited) arrangements. Ms F had felt that the session had been OK, a good thing for the sake of the children. An agreement was made for contact to begin on a set date and then to proceed on a weekly basis. Both parties agree that the arrangements lasted only two weeks. Ms F explains:

> My husband didn't feel the contact suitable and now doesn't see the children at all. As he is alcohol-dependent, I have mixed feelings - I would prefer him to have contact for everyone's sake but the aggravation and worry attached is a huge concern.

She adds that nothing else could have been done at mediation in order to preserve the agreement because of the 'alcohol factor'. In contrast, Mr F felt that arrangements had been undermined because:

> My wife wanted to go away with the children...she wished to use them as a financial weapon,

and that more could have been done at mediation, a prior meeting with both parties perhaps. He also suggests that the views of the children might have been sought and offers the following idea in conclusion:

> The court order should be enforceable. As a father with three daughters under 16 the police did not want to know.

# Index